Petit Apartheid in the U.S. Criminal Justice System

Petit Apartheid in the U.S. Criminal Justice System

The Dark Figure of Racism

Dragan Milovanovic
Northeastern Illinois University

Katheryn K. Russell
University of Maryland

Carolina Academic Press
Durham, North Carolina

Library of Congress Cataloging-in-Publication Data

Milovanovic, Dragan, date.
    Petit apartheid in criminal justice / Dragan Milovanovic, Katheryn K.
    Russell.
        p. cm.
    Includes bibliographical references and index.
    ISBN 0-89089-951-7
    1. Discrimination in criminal justice administration--United States. 2.
Racial profiling in law enforcement--United States. 3. Crime and race--
United States. I. Russell, Katheryn K., 1961 - II. Title.

HV9950 .M56 2001
364'.089'96073--dc21

                                                                2001028013

Carolina Academic Press
700 Kent Street
Durham, North Carolina 27701
Telephone (919) 489-7486
Fax (919) 493-5668
E-mail: cap@cap-press.com
www.cap-press.com

Printed in the United States of America.

Contents

Preface

This book arose from numerous conversations that we had over the last few years concerning Daniel Georges-Abeyie's notion of petit apartheid. These conversations took place at the annual meetings of the American Society of Criminology. We were convinced that the idea needed further development and that we should do a co-edited book on the subject. We were intrigued with the notion that macro-level forms of racism exist along with informal, more invisible forms. These micro-level aggressions remain a "dark figure," but surely contribute, be it in a cumulative form, to the continued assaults made on African Americans. The term "dark figure" is typically used to refer to crime that is not included in official justice statistics. We use the term to refer to racially-motivated processes within the justice system that, heretofore, have escaped official recordkeeping, thus analysis. And all too often these "microaggressions" discriminate and place at risk African Americans before the law. We also realized that the micro level plays itself out at the macro, and the macro at the micro, a cycle which sustains hierarchy and harms of reductions and repression. We were determined to do further investigations. Subsequently, we organized two panels on the subject at the 1999 American Society of Criminology meetings. These aroused much discussion. (On our own campuses we had occasions to organize discussions which were well attended, lively and illuminating.) We then asked the paper presenters to contribute to our book on the same subject. The end result was this book.

All the contributors were excited about what the book could potentially do for social change. It was our hope that this book, by making visible these various forms of petit apartheid, would encourage critical scholars to do further research in the area. We certainly hope that new methodologies and creative energies will be brought to bear in this important area.

Dragan Milovanovic
Northeastern Illinois University

Katheryn K. Russell
University of Maryland

Foreword

Petit Apartheid in Criminal Justice: "The More 'Things' Change, the More 'Things' Remain the Same"

Daniel E. Georges-Abeyie

How frequently has one heard the phrase "The more 'things' change, the more 'things' remain the same." Perhaps too frequently, perhaps too often? Ten years ago, I had the honor to write a series of essays that were published in Brian D. MacLean and Dragan Milovanovic's *Racism, Empiricism and Criminal Justice* (1990). In that book I coined the concept of "petit apartheid in criminal justice." This was done in response to a disturbing challenge to reason and historical fact offered in Professor William Wilbanks' book, *The Myth of a Racist Criminal Justice System* (1987). Wilbanks' book was perceived to be the rebirth of the Michael J. Hindelang's thesis—one that rationalized what he and other conservative criminologists correctly believed to be the disproportionality of Uniform Crime Report's "Part-One Index" crimes by so-called "Blacks," while it incorrectly alleged the lenient criminal justice "system" treatment of Blacks being prosecuted. Wilbank's conclusion was based upon society's (including the criminal justice system's) devaluation of the inherent worth of "Black" lives—a devaluation that criminologists fail to discuss in detail. In fact, this devaluation necessitates an in-depth analysis of the offender-victim dynamic—one which is sensitive to the complexity of Black ethnicity and the spatial morphology of offending.

I stated ten years ago that a reasonable analysis of so-called "Black" crime needs the following: (1) a spatial context in which so-called Black rates of offending are identified throughout the spatial morphology of the non-ghetto, ghetto, and slum-ghetto; (2) an ethnically-sophisticated context in which differential rates of offending are noted by, and within, the Negroid ethnic context such as Afro-Hispanic (e.g., Puerto Rican, Dominican, Cuban, Panamanian), Afro-Caribbean Anglophone (e.g., Jamaican, Trinidadian), Afro-Caribbean-Transitional (e.g., Virgin Island, Belizean, Gullah), and African-American (by region and urban/rural context as well as by maroon/non-maroon context); and (3) a "petit apartheid"/"grand apartheid" contextual analysis—one sensitive to "second-hand" criminality as a response to the weight of negative social factors and discretionary decision-making by both criminal justice agents and criminal justice agencies. These discretionary actions are often transformed or transmuted into discrimination. Thus, they produce the distortion of official rates of offending by Blacks and other minorities (over reporting) as well as by majority race offenders (under reporting), due to non-system handling of apparently criminally offensive behavior.

In the McLean and Milovanovic book, *Racism, Empiricism and Criminal Justice*, I referred to the "informal," de facto mores and norms, i.e., culturally biased beliefs and actions that permeate the American criminal justice "system" and result in discretion being transmuted into discrimination as "petit apartheid" realities. I knew then, as I know now, that social distance between alleged offenders, suspects, detainees, and defendants, and the law enforcement establishment, officers of the court, and correctional/jail/detention staff and correctional/jail/detention administrators—all dramatically impact on the decision-making process. I have witnessed with certitude:

> [T]he everyday slights, insults, rough or brutal treatment and unnecessary stops, questions, and searches of blacks; the lack of civility faced by black suspects/arrestees[/detainees]: the quality, clarity, and objectivity of the judges' instructions to the jury when a black arrestee is on trial; the acceptance of lesser standards of evidence in cases that result in the conviction of black arrestees[/defendants], as well as numerous other punitively discretionary acts by law enforcement and correctional[jail/detention] officers as well as jurists (Georges-Abeyie, 1990:12).

To the previously cited occurrences of "petit apartheid" in criminal justice—in which Blacks are treated more harshly when Blacks are defendants involved in the alleged victimization of Whites—I now, ten years later, add the bizarre convoluted forms of criminal justice processing (i.e., lenient sentencing, the *nolle prosequi*, remands to state mental health facilities, and jury nullification in cases that involve White defendants and Black victims). I denounce these abominable practices and reiterate the necessity of observing and analyzing these practices if one is to understand the transmuting reality of "petit apartheid in criminal justice."

I observe with horror how "The more things change, the more things remain the same." Consider some examples: (1) In 1984, Bernhard Goetz shot four alleged would-be robbers on a subway in New York City and received almost no punishment for his violent acts; (2) In 1991, following the police beating of Rodney King in Los Angeles, the L.A. District Attorney Ira Reiner called the behavior of the officers who watched, "irresponsible and offensive, but not criminal." The officers charged in the King beating were found "not guilty," (e.g., jury nullification); (3) See also the "change of venue" permitted in the Amadou Diallo case; (4) Note the lenient sentence assigned officers in the Abner Louima case. These late 1990s cases may have signaled an even more virulent manifestation of "petit apartheid in criminal justice," and; (5) We have seen the muted rationalization of excessive use of force when Philadelphia Police Commissioner John F. Timoney addressed the police (Arizona Republic 2000) following the police beating and kicking of a car jacking suspect. Timoney stated that he would not "rush to judgment" on the proprietary of the police action based upon a news helicopter videotape of the incident.

As a son of a Gullah/Geechee mother and a Caribbean father of Virgin Island/Panamanian/Puerto Rican/Cuban heritage I watched with horror and fascination the bifurcated demon of apartheid on two continents. "Petit apartheid in criminal justice" was rationalized again and again. I became involved with the African National Congress of South Africa as a youth before it was popular or politically correct. I wrote articles under a pseudonym for its political organ—*Sechaba*—and was branded a communist, a terrorist, and a rebel, labels I bore and brandished with pride. I also joined and supported several left-of-center political parties in the U.S. that condemned what I called "grand apartheid" in the Republic of South Africa and Black Codes/Jim Crow in the U.S. I knew by heart the bloody birth and progression of "grand apartheid" and its subsequent slow miserable death abroad in my adopted home. I knew of its birth in 1948 (also the year of my birth), when the National Party came to power. And then I applauded its death.

The demise resulted in: (1) the relaxation of occupational restrictions and segregation in employment in the late 1970s and 1980s; (2) the repeal of the 1948 law that forbade interracial marriage/miscegenation; (3) the repeal of the pass laws in 1985; (4) the creation of the Constitution of 1983 that gave Coloureds and Asians, but not Blacks, limited representation in the formerly all-White national parliament; (5) the June 1991 repeal of the Group Areas Act of 1966 and the Land Acts of 1913 and 1936; (6) the 1991 repeal of the Population Registration Act of 1950; (7) the 1994 reincorporation of the homelands (the Black Bantustans) into the Republic of South Africa under an interim post-apartheid constitution adopted in 1993; and (8) the 1994 election in which 12 of the 19 major parties pictured nonwhite candidates on the national ballot. In the latter election, the African National Congress and its South African allies, including the South African Communist Party, established parliamentary power "parliamentarily."

I knew in 1991, as I knew in 1994, as I do today, that *de jure* racism transmutes into de facto racism and that criminal justice practices and procedures once enshrined via de jure oppression, transformed into discrimination under the guise of discretion. That is, "grand apartheid" would transmute into "petit apartheid"—oppressive laws into mores and customs. The U.S. experienced a similar metamorphosis. Thus, why would, or should the experience of oppressed Blacks in the Republic of South Africa be different than that of Blacks in the U.S.?

The conventional sociological theories of "structural-functionalism" and "cognitive dissonance" bestowed a lesson upon me: the knowledge that structural manifestations (i.e., behaviors) remain long after the original reason for their origin, and that if one should desire to permanently change a belief—cognition—one needs to change behavior first. I learned that one has to get persons to choose the desired behaviors because of perceived benefits. Only then can the desired behavior be rationalized and result in cognition change.

The reason for "grand apartheid" in the U.S. (e.g., slavery, Black Codes, and Jim Crow Law) or in the Republic of South Africa, and the reason for "petit apartheid," is one and the same. It benefits and advantages some people. This "advantage" is enacted into law, issued via court findings and/or executive decrees (e.g., executive order). The reality of "petit apartheid in criminal justice" remains the reality of advantage, and thus, the subordination of some by others. The reality of "petit apartheid" is not always the overt conscious act of a subjugating agent who knowingly brutalizes the subjugated, although it too often is. The core reality of "petit apartheid" remains advantage, and thus, disadvantage.

The key to understanding "petit apartheid" in criminal justice is to understand the reality of actual outcome, not to fixate on alleged intent. Petit apartheid continues to manifest itself in both subtle and overt ways. It can, and has appeared in the vertical promotion of White officers and in the horizontal promotion (e.g., special assignment without promotion or remuneration) of Black officers and other minority officers. It can, and has been manifested in the police use of excessive force by both minority and majority race officers against Black and other minority race/ethnicity suspects and detainees. It is also manifest by the fact that majority race officers believe that they can engage in overtly illegal and brutal behavior—such as the horrific, violent sodomizing and beating of a Black suspect/arrestee in confines of a police precinct house in New York City, as was the case with Abner Louima.

Petit apartheid can, and has been manifested in jury nullification, in cases that involve police officers who have brutalized Blacks and other low status racial/ethnic minorities. Jury nullification has classically been the action of civilians ignoring evidence and the determination of guilt based upon the legal concept of "beyond a reasonable doubt" in order to convict Black and other minority race/ethnic defendants accused of the victimization of Whites or other high status individuals, while returning a finding of not guilty when the defendant is White and the victim Negroid (e.g., the Amadou Diallo case).

It can, and has been manifested in racial/ethnic profiling of suspects that has, and continues to result in selective stops and searches along the border, at airports, at customs stations, and at traffic stops, or by "neighborhood watch" interventions or by beat patrol by uniformed and plain cloth officers. For example, a June 29, 2000 announcement by the U.S. Custom Services is instructive. It announced an intent to change its racial and ethnic profiling policy that resulted in the disproportionate (without merit) stop, frisk, and strip searches of Black females.

It can, and has been manifested in the selectively more punitive enforcement of departmental rules and regulations when allegedly violated by Black and other minority race/ethnicity officers or agents of the court. Examples of this are detailed in my edited book, *The Criminal Justice System and Blacks* (Part 2)(1984).

I have frequently wondered when it would again be my turn to suffer the indignities of "petit apartheid in criminal justice." I have wondered as I breathed within "my suit" of dark brown skin, when I would be stopped, frisked, and questioned, and possibly interned in an INS facility as I pled my "Americanism," my "nationality," my belonging here in "America," especially given my "foreign" sounding name, "Daniel E. Georges-Abeyie." I know that "grand apartheid" died in the U.S. with the issuance of executive orders (e.g., Executive Order 91, which officially desegregated the U.S. military) and the enactment of the Thirteenth, Fourteenth, and Fifteenth Amendments, as well as with U.S. Supreme Court decisions leading up to *McCleskey v. Kemp* (481 U.S. 279, 1987).

In brief, I am pleased that Drs. Dragan Milovanovic and Katheryn K. Russell have chosen to edit this new volume on petit apartheid in criminal justice. It is a volume much needed on a topic bizarrely ignored as social scientists have chosen to focus on overt racism in criminal justice: "grand apartheid," indeed, an increasingly rare anachronism. However, official acts of discrimination and multivariate analysis are data and research techniques well-suited to today's "publish or perish" world of academe. "Grand apartheid" may be quickly observed and the data easily manipulated for multivariate analysis not necessarily grounded in the knowledge of the culture of the "victim."

The analysis of "petit apartheid," however, is best served by grounded theory, participant observation studies, and open-ended interview guides, although multivariate analysis can document differentials in sentences and some punitive actions by justice agencies when the race and the ethnicity of subjects are allegedly "known." Thus, there certainly is a place for multivariate analysis and the study of overt racism and to a lesser extent the study of new manifestations of "grand apartheid" draped under the guise of objective testing criteria and enhanced sentencing guidelines and salient factor scores.

Nonetheless, the interpretation of the law during jury instructions, the inflection of the voice, the body language of a police officer or of an officer of the court, the raising of an eyebrow, and the penetrating gaze or scow of a judge will never be captured by multivariate analysis — yet, they are as real as any gun or knife that wounds or kills. Non-verbal and verbal exchanges and cues by criminal justice agents, noted in my own writings (1981; 1984; 1989; 1990; 1992) and in the writings of others, such as Russell (1998) and Davis (1989), need to be studied and explained. The findings in the Rodney King, Amadou Diallo, Bernard Goetz, and Abner Louima cases are not mysteries to the authors of this volume. Each sensitively portrays the various guises of "petit apartheid" in criminal justice.

I have read the writings of the authors in this volume. Each in her/his own way illuminates the more covert, hidden forms of discrimination. It is my hope that this volume will result in a serious examination of the spatial dimension of so-called "Black" crime in its "petit apartheid" forms.

Cases Cited

McCleskey v. Kemp, 481 U.S. 279 (1987).

Introduction

Petit Apartheid

Dragan Milovanovic and Katheryn K. Russell

Research on racial disparity has been catalogued into four periods or "waves" (Zatz 1987). During the first period, 1930-1960, most studies found clear evidence of criminal justice system bias against minorities. In the second wave, 1960-1970, many concluded there was little evidence of overt racial discrimination. In the third period, 1970-1980, researchers determined that racial discrimination had taken on newer, more subtle forms. Since the 1980s, however, the mainstream view has been that the criminal justice system is not marked by formal discrimination (see the series of discussions directed against Wilbank's "no discrimination thesis" [in B. MacLean and D. Milovanovic (eds.), *Racism, Empiricism and Criminal Justice* (1990)].

During this same period, however, a growing number of researchers have argued that the "informal" stages of the justice system must be included in any analysis of racial discrimination. Georges-Abeyie (1990) has argued that the discriminatory and discretionary actions of police officers during the informal stages, such as pre-arrest, result in "petit apartheid" (Ibid.). These are various forms of indignities, insults, put-downs, and belittling action directed towards Blacks. Russell (1998) has referred to these as "microaggressions" (see also Davis 1989). These informal stages can also have cumulative and interactional effects. This book includes a collection of articles on petit apartheid and how it is affected by race, class, gender, and also by their intersections (Crenshaw 1989, 1993; Collins 1993; Milovanovic and Schwartz 1999). In other words, race, gender, and class discrimination often appear in various configurations with unequal weight often attached to one of the three. One factor, for example, could be, in context, the dominant one.

A critical analysis that makes visible petit apartheid practices draws us away from traditional paradigms in law and criminology. Donald Black (1989), for example, has argued for a critical sociological paradigm rather than the limited jurisprudential model (e.g., legal formalism). His approach — the "sociology of the case" — sees law as a quantitative variable varying in time and space. His primary variables are "status" and the consideration of "each adversary's social status in relation to the other's" (Ibid., 9). He further specifies another component as "relational distance" that has much to do with the micro-sociological constructions that may discriminate against the disenfranchised. In this same direction, Ewick and Silbey (1998) have offered a paradigm focused on the "social construction of legality" which focuses on cultural practices. In *Words That Wound*, Matsuda, Lawrence, Delgado, and Crenshaw advocate a critical race theory, "a jurisprudence in/of color" (Matsuda 1996, 21), a component of which "challenges a historicism and insists on a contextual/historical analysis of the law" (Matsuda et al. 1993, 6). This paradigm is from a victim's perspective, from the experience of subordination.

All this, too, entails an alternative definition of harm in criminal justice. The legalistic definition has conveniently overlooked other forms of harm. One alternative (Henry and Milovanovic 1996), rooted in postmodern thought, is the constitutive definition of harm: "harms of reduction" and "harms of repression." "*Harms of reduction* occur when an offended party experiences a loss of some quality relative to their present standing; *harms of repression* occur when an offended party experiences a limit or restriction preventing them from achieving a desired position or standing" (1996, 103). Accordingly, "these are harms either because they move the offended away from a position or state they currently occupy, or because they prevent them from occupying a position or state that they desire" (Ibid.). Petit apartheid practices, as we will see from the chapters which follow, are harms of reduction and harms of repression which are not captured in the official legalistic definition of crime. They are harmful in two senses: they belittle, demean, ridicule or subordinate on the one hand, and on the other, they limit access to equal opportunities and fair dealings before the law, i.e., DWB (driving while Black), SWB (standing while Black), RWB (running while Black).

At the macro-sociological level of analysis ("grand apartheid"), many convincing studies have indicated the various forms of discrimination that exist. Surely, structural factors (e.g., economic, political) should be one target for change (see the case for the existence of "black genocide" by Johnson and Leighton 1995, and for the existence of "cultural violence" by Oliver, forthcoming). However, at the micro level—the everyday encounters of humans in interaction and communication —there is also a need to develop creative change strategies in situations where petit apartheid arises. Structure and consciousness are only separable analytically; in truth, each exists in the other as critical race theory (Crenshaw 1993, 111-132), the constitutive theory (Henry and Milovanovic, 1996), and others (Ewick and Silbey 1998) have argued.

Several suggestions in the literature have been made as to how to deal with everyday instances of harm (petit apartheid). Ewick and Silbey's (1998) insightful analysis of the semiotic constructions of legalities in everyday life has indicated how reversals of the trajectories of power can emerge by which, for a moment, opposition, resistance, liberation, and autonomy can take place. Similarly, Henry and Milovanovic (1996) have offered the "social judo" metaphor by which harm can be used against itself without the resort to furthering overall violence.

We find one example in the contemporary movement in placing video cameras in police cars. Police officers, whose everyday interactions with motorists, for example, have remained invisible and asymetrical, now will have their actions subject to the scrutiny of the public, researchers, and activists. What was previously the asymetrical use of power has now undergone the democratic movement toward symmetry. Research awaits on how (media) staging of "stops," "frisks," and "searches" (a "backstage" area made "frontstage" — see Chapter 1 by Katheryn K. Russell) will be conducted. Which is to say that the dialectics of struggle must also be confronted as we inadvertently extend the disciplinary powers of panopticism (Foucault 1977).[1] Exploding these stereotypes has been suggested as another strategy. This may be a double-edged sword. Crenshaw's critical analysis of 2 Live Crew, for example, suggests that "exploding stereotypes" as a strategy for overcoming racism (i.e., the use of racial stereotypes and of "sexual hyperbole" to evoke laughter), although plausible in the abstract, may "do more to reinforce and entrench the [stereotype] image than to explode it" (1993, 128). Yet another strategy is providing moments whereby nonconfrontational space is opened to talk about race, gender, and class discrimination (Matsuda 1996, 124-129). In these Freirian encounters

> students told funny but troubling stories of mistaken identity. A Black or Chicano man in a tux is asked for an ashtray or a glass of water at a formal event. A woman in a law firm is subject to the assumption that she is there to type and take messages (Ibid., 125).

In these encounters of student and teacher interchange, awareness, respect, and understanding of the other develop, and a critical, humanistic consciousness is raised.

But all this is for further research. Surely this important line of research in dealing with petit apartheid will be pursued further. The chapters in this book, not only are enlightening as to the occurrence of petit apartheid, but are also suggestive as to further research in this area.

Petit apartheid practices, therefore, must begin to be analyzed from a more interdisciplinary, holistic approach. This book is a beginning attempt to make visible these forms of harms and is suggestive as to further critical scholarly investigations. In this investigation we are in need of an understanding of the various dimensions of petit apartheid. Daniel Georges-Abeyie, for example, has specified the nature of petit apartheid: it consists of

> ...the everyday insults, rough or brutal treatment, and unnecessary stops, questions, and searches of blacks; the lack of civility faced by black suspects/arrestees; the quality, clarity, and objectivity of the judges' instructions to the jury when a black arrestee is on trial; the acceptance of lesser standards of evidence in cases that result in the conviction of black arrestees, as well as numerous other punitively discretionary acts by law enforcement and correctional officers as well as jurists (1990, 12).

He therefore implies that petit apartheid practices appear at all levels of the criminal justice system, from pre-arrest, through trial proceedings, and at post conviction stages. Thus, we could portray these moments in the following table (see also Chapter 1 by Katheryn K. Russell). We stress that these are only preliminary typologies meant more as a stimulus for further research on the more subtle, more covert forms of racism.

One framework, "Continuum: Petit Apartheid," could look at petit apartheid's location on a continuum from the more covert and informal forms to the more overt, formal forms (see Table 1, below). Thus, at one end, perhaps the most hidden, are the non-verbal gestures, postures, mannerisms as well as omissions that are found in everyday interactions. It includes "crimes of style" (Ferrell, 1996) — insignia, clothing, and other symbolic paraphenalia which become the basis of disrespectful behavior of law enforcement. It would also include the phenomenon of internalized petit apartheid whereby the responses to law enforcement might include self belittling, subordinating self, excessive deference, and the arousal of fear, the cumulative results of which maintain hegemonic hierarchical relations of power inequality and harm. The chapters by Douglas Thompkins and Jackie Campbell highlight some of these.

Further along the continuum we may envision verbal, but unofficial actions by law enforcement officials. These include the unrecorded discourses of hate, insults and disrespect and include implicit or explicit discourse which suggests or outright states that "you don't belong here." The chapter by Lee Ross suggests some of the reasons why African Americans do not pursue law enforcement careers. The chapter by Jeff Ferrell also presents examples of the creation of cultural spaces and differential risk.

Next along our continuum, moving toward the "Overt/Formal" forms of discrimination, are discriminatory practices that are more action (behavioral) oriented, which result in harms of reductions and repression. Driving, standing, and running while Black, for example, all place some at higher risk of official police intervention. This also includes the differential standards applied in the criminal justice system even though, on the face of it, formal law was ostensibly being applied. Thus arrest, bail, sentencing, and death penalty decisions have all been shown to have race effects. Jeannete Covington's chapter brings out many examples.

Further along the continuum are the official legal discourses and legal social constructions of reality invoked by law enforcement, which nevertheless are selective and in many cases are *ex post facto* constructions. Instructions to juries and the legal social constructions of the Miranda warnings, plain view doctrine, grounds provided for stops, frisks and searches, and prosecutor's closing arguments to the jury are moments where these forms of discrimination are pronounced. Sheri Lee Johnson's chapter presents many enlightening examples.

And finally, the most overt and formal moments of discrimination, are policies, such as those of the Highland Park Police of Illinois, whereby minorities are targeted for vehicle stops under the rationale that they have greater criminal propensities even in the face of clear evidence indicating that these disproportional "criminal propensities" by race do not surface. The chapters by Sandra Bass and Jeannette Covington address these issues.

Georges-Abeyie also calls for the development of a grounded theory: "Such a grounded theoretical approach might also note the significance of 'petit Apartheid' victimizations (i.e., indignities) that go unreported, and thus undocumented, yet nonetheless indelibly impact upon community/police relations and expectations" (1990, 32). Here, there is much to be done. The "dark figure" (e.g., the invisible, covert, hidden figure) of petit apartheid remains an area for creative theorizing in bringing out an alternative methodology which makes it visible. Criticizing Wilbank's "no discrimination thesis," Georges-Abeyie has said: "His [Wilbank's] analysis . . . also lacks a spatial sophistication that might be cognizant of racial and ethnic bias by jurors and judges when crimes occur within specific ecological zones of the alleged ghetto, slum-ghetto, or non-ghetto" (1990, 13, 32). Here, culturally sensitive scholars need to develop instruments that more accurately measure the subtle forms of petit apartheid.

A further development of the notion of petit apartheid is implied by Davis (1989) and Russell (1998). These "microaggressions" consist of racial assaults that are "subtle, stunning, often automatic and nonverbal exchanges which are 'put downs' of Blacks [by Whites]" (cited in Russell 1998, 138). Russell (1998, 138-139) provides the following example:

> A White person who refuses to hold an elevator for a Black person, a White person who will not make direct eye contact with a Black person while speaking to him, a White person who enters a business office and assumes that the Black person she sees is a sec-

Table 1—Continuum: Petit Apartheid

COVERT/INFORMAL	------------> DISCRIMINATORY PRACTICES ------------>			OVERT/FORMAL
Non-verbal	Verbal ("unofficial")	Action	Verbal ("official")	Verbal + Action
Gestures, postures, mannerisms; omissions; civility not offered; presumption of "second class citizen" rank; non-person status; disrespect; internalized automatic responses to law enforcement agents that belittle, subordinate, engender fear, and dehumanize; hegemonic reproduction of power relations due to excessive deference; "crimes of style" (i.e., insignia, clothing, etc.).	(No "official" verbal action). Put downs, fighting words, expletives, hate/racist, speech, insults; messages/ discourses of hate and racial inferiority (i.e., "Hey Boy!"); spatial exclusions ("you don't belong here!").	Informal racial profiling: DWB, RWB, SWB; police everyday work practices; acting out stereotypes in "stops" and "searches"; race as a proxy for dangerousness, and hence for differential law enforcement; reliance on lesser standards for conviction; less likely to receive bail; greater chance in being recipient of deadly force; more likely to be jailed and receive death penalty when victim is white.	Invocation of selective discourse of law ("official" action); reliance on official words of law; legal social constructions; instructions to jury; ex post facto constructions of plain view doctrine, grounds for stops/ arrest, etc; prosecutor's biased closing argument to the jury.	Formal racial profiling (i.e., Highland Pk, Il. police); loitering laws (Chicago); injunctions vs. alleged gang members and affiliating in public (California); gang profiles and renunciation requirements before release; selective drug laws and discretionary enforcement.

retary or a janitor, a cab driver who refuses to pick up a Black passenger, a White person who refuses to give directions to someone Black, and a White sales clerk who offers assistance to a White patron in line behind a Black patron.

In short, petit apartheid and microaggressions represent a more invisible dimension in discussions of race and criminal justice. Our book will make visible these forms of discrimination and indicate how investigations of racism in the criminal justice system must be expanded to the more informal levels of interactions. Accordingly, our first chapter by Katheryn K. Russell entitled "Toward Developing a Theoretical Paradigm and Typology for Petit Apartheid," develops the initial strokes for a typology of petit apartheid. It suggests theoretical directions for investigating these more subtle, more covert, invisible forms of discrimination. It is a call for placing petit apartheid practices under a sociological umbrella.

The next two book chapters provide personal introductions to the practice of petit apartheid. Chapter 2 by Jackie Campbell, entitled "Walking the Beat Alone: An African American Police Officer's Perspective on Petit Apartheid," concerns a personal experience by a female African-American police sergeant in a large metropolitan police department. It indicates how a culture of prejudice exists which produces discriminatory and stereotypical behaviors by police officers. It indicates how Black youths in particular are at risk of police interventions. Chapter 3 by Doug Thompkins, entitled "The Presence and Effect of Micro-Aggressions and Petit Apartheid," indicates how he and other Black men often develop defensive mechanisms to avoid intimidating White people in everyday street encounters. He reflects on other aspects of petit apartheid. Here petit apartheid is turned inward. He questions what is to be done.

In Chapter 4, Jeannette Covington's article, "Round Up the Usual Suspects: Racial Profiling and the War on Drugs," focuses on informal decision-making. It underscores how stereotypical behaviors become commonplace in police departments. It shows how Black youth are at high risk of suspicion when there is an outbreak of crime. And it shows how racial profiling at both the formal and informal levels produce high rates of official action directed toward Blacks. The chapter systematically indicates, by the use of statistics, that the at-risk population is not necessarily the disproportionally crime-producing population. Finally, it exposes the connection between racial profiling and drug scares.

Chapter 5 by Sandra Bass, entitled "Out of Place: Petit Apartheid and the Police," focuses on discretionary decision-making by police. She argues that the interaction between minorities and police is an apartheid-like relationship. This is especially acute in gang-identification practices by police. These lead to wide sweeps in inner city neighborhoods and most often include innocent people. These are indignities continuously suffered. The police stress on "quality of life" forms of behavior offer wide latitude for police invocations of stops, frisks, and arrests.

Jeff Ferrell, in Chapter 6, entitled "Trying to Make Us a Parking Lot: Petit Apartheid, Cultural Spaces, and the Public Negotiation of Ethnicity," continues with Sandra Bass's theme in indicating how with "urban redevelopment" cultural spaces become increasingly differentiated for police intrusions. His postmodern/cultural studies approach indicates how spatial arrangements develop with symbolic meaning, some of which become overly targeted for police action. It is here where petit apartheid practices are ubiquitous but remain beyond the oversight of public bodies. As cases-in-point, he offers commentary on three cultural contexts: street cruisers and lowriders; hip-hop graffiti; and gangs, loitering, and gang injunctions. In each case, petit apartheid practices are omnipresent. He also suggests cultural styles of oppositional practices.

Lee Ross, in Chapter 7, entitled "African American Interest in Law Enforcement: A Consequence of Petit Apartheid?" addresses the question of why more African Americans do not enter law enforcement professions. Of particular importance is the question of when does an identification turn from Black to Blue? He argues that the contemporary, widespread discourse in criminal justice concerning Black crime dissuades many African American undergraduates from pursuing careers in law enforcement. This abandonment, however, leaves criminal justice predominantly in the hands of those least likely to be exposed to discriminatory and oppressive law enforcement practices. Pressure, however, such as accusations of "selling out," militate further against African Americans pursuing law enforcement careers. Ultimately, the dilemma of Black turning to Blue identification assures a form of hegemony that comes full circle in placing African Americans at risk before the law. It is often the case, Ross argues, that petit apartheid practices produce this climate of abandonment and conversion.

Finally, in Chapter 8, Sheri Lynn Johnson's article, "Racial Derogation in Prosecutors' Closing Arguments," posits that petit apartheid practices become the basis of many closing arguments. She argues that racial imagery is conveyed in the structure of stories, metaphors, selective pictures, and examples provided during closing arguments to juries. It is here where stereotypes are presented and where fears are exploited. Race often becomes more hidden and more covert in the presentational styles of lawyers; it is allowed to play itself out in innuendos, suggestions, metaphors, implications, and examples. It is also disheartening to see, that at the appellate level, obvious racial imageries conjured up in summation are often allowed to stand. Such doctrines as "harmless error" and "plain error" are constructed and practiced such that biased summations do not deter racial imagery. To correct some of these practices, Johnson suggests a definition for negative "racial imagery," a standard which could be the basis of appeal in cases of prosecutors' racial prejudices in closing arguments.

In sum, the chapters included in this book, by focusing on different dimensions of petit apartheid, bring to light what has often remained invisible. The "dark figure" of petit apartheid occurences has yet to be quantified. Nevertheless, its cumulative effect continues to produce harms of repression and reduction. It is our hope that this book will lead to the development of further analysis of this dimension of discrimination. Of particular concern should also be how to deal effectively with everyday petit apartheid occurrences.

Endnote

1. The dialectics of struggle can take many forms. We must always be prepared to counter unproductive forms of struggle such as political correctness, reversal of hierarchies (hierarchy still remains), hate politics (Cornell 1999), and exorcism (e.g., the overzealous "reformer" who is too quick in constructing the evil in the other, despite counter evidence, and thereafter attacks his/her own constructions under the banner of doing good).

Petit Apartheid in the U.S. Criminal Justice System

1

Toward Developing a Theoretical Paradigm and Typology for Petit Apartheid

Katheryn K. Russell

Introduction

There is nothing new about the ceiling-high rates of arrest, conviction, and incarceration of Blacks in the United States. For more than a century, Blacks who comprise approximately 12 percent of the population, have accounted for *at least* 20 percent of the population held under the control of the nation's criminal justice system. In fact, rates of racial disparity continue to inch upward. All manner of explanations—theoretical, legal, historical, and empirical—have been offered to explain this trend. Race-based laws (*de jure* and *de facto*), which singled out Blacks for special treatment, are one identifiable root of this disparity. The United States' historical record indicates that Blacks have long been singled out for harsh legal treatment, pre and post-slavery. In some instances, the law has expressly sanctioned differential treatment by race (e.g., slave codes, Black codes, and Jim Crow). In others, the criminal justice system *process* has enabled differential treatment to take place.

Daniel Georges-Abeyie refers to the former scheme as "grand apartheid" and the later as "petit apartheid" (see Foreword). The harms and mechanisms of a system that explicitly denotes and sanctions an "inferior" race are manifest. In fact, such clear indicia of racial bias are no longer legal. What remains hidden are the myriad ways that covert racial discrimination operates within the justice system, and the harm it causes. Mainstream criminologists have made few attempts to operationalize, quantify, and analyze these processes and their affects. Thus, the cost of this parallel form of discrimination has largely escaped empirical measure and assessment, and remedy. The locations and mechanisms of this remaining form of racial discrimination are the focus of this chapter. The analysis demonstrates that

3

discriminatory policies and practices persist within the criminal justice system.

"Petit Apartheid"

Scores of researchers have evaluated the impact of race on the criminal justice system (e.g., Kennedy 1997, Miller 1996, Tonry 1995, Blumstein 1993, Mann 1993, and Wilbanks 1987). These analyses are oft-times divided into two categories, those which conclude that discrimination exists ("Discrimination Thesis") and those which conclude race discrimination does not exist ("No Discrimination Thesis") (MacLean and Milovanovic 1990). Daniel Georges-Abeyie, whose analysis falls into the former camp, argues that there are routine, identifiable practices and places within the criminal justice system where racial discrimination festers (1990). These systemic racial cracks guarantee that a disproportionate number of African Americans are trapped within the criminal justice system's net. Georges-Abeyie labels the totality of this process "petit apartheid." He describes it this way:

> Does the focus of the criminal justice analysis on the formal, easily observed decision-making process obscure or even misdirect attention from the most significant contemporary form of racism within the criminal justice system? [For example,] the everyday insults, rough or brutal treatment, and unnecessary stops, questions, and searches of blacks; the lack of civility faced by black suspects/arrestees; the quality, clarity, and objectivity of the judge's instructions to the jury when a black arrestee is on trial; the acceptance of lesser standards of evidence in cases that result in the conviction of black arrestees, as well as numerous other punitively discretionary acts by law enforcement and correctional officers as well as jurists (Georges-Abeyie 1990, 12).

Unfortunately, it is difficult to dispute Georges-Abeyie's conclusion that race affects each stage of the judicial system. It might be tempting, initially, to dismiss his use of "apartheid" — a term typically limited to describing an overtly racist political regime — as hyperbole. However, even the most cursory review of the U.S. justice system presents a sobering picture, one in which Blackness and crime are inextricably linked.

In fact, the practices identified by Georges-Abeyie, such as "unnecessary stops," undergird past and present race-based challenges to police and judicial system practices. For example, the incidence and prevalence of racial profiling have received continental and international attention (U.S. Department of State 1999, Ogletree 2000). Specifically, concerns have been raised that Blacks—young, Black men in particular—are unfairly targeted for sanction by the justice system—at every step, from arrest to parole. The public discussion of racial targeting has primarily focused on vehicle stops where "Blackness" has been used as an indicator of criminality. This practice, also known as "Driving While Black," has been the subject of congressional and state investigation, and federal and state legislation (e.g., U.S. Commission on Civil Rights 2000, Government Accounting Office 2000, Harris 1999, and Russell 1998).

Georges-Abeyie argues that racial profiling is but one in a long line of practices which position Blacks in the cross hairs of the justice system. At core, the operating systems of the U.S. criminal justice system create and reinforce racially-segregated outcomes. Georges-Abeyie's thesis acknowledges the interplay between the formal and informal stages of the criminal justice system. Formal stages are those which are subject to official record-keeping and analysis (e.g., arrest, sentencing) and the informal stages are those which are not (e.g., pre-arrest, closing arguments). The petit apartheid framework exposes the *processes* that consistently prescribe punitive outcomes for Blacks, at each stage of the justice system.

A vast body of research examines the impact of race at various stages of the criminal justice system. For example, single stage analyses include evaluations of the impact of race on arrest, prosecutorial charge, and sentencing. The literature also includes research which investigates the impact of race using a multi-stage analysis (two or more), such as prosecutorial charging and sentencing. It has become increasingly clear, however, that the research methods for evaluating this problem are inadequate (e.g., Russell 1998, 26-33).

A focus on the formal stages of the justice system, by definition, means that the activity that occurs at the informal stages have not been considered. Thus, an accurate assessment of whether and how race-based outcomes occur must include a review beyond the formal stages. As critical, existing analyses have failed to examine the relationship between and across formal and informal stages.

This chapter, which takes a step toward filling this analytical void, has four objectives. First, to place Georges-Abeyie's thesis within a historical and theoretical framework. Second, to map out the how-when-where of petit apartheid. The typology identifies the sites and mechanisms which systematically introduce more Blacks into the criminal justice system than any other racial group. Third, to explicate the key constituent parts of this typology. Finally, to assess the impact of our failure to address racial tracking in the U.S. justice system.

Theoretical Overview: Placing Petit Apartheid
Under a Sociological Umbrella

This section constructs a theoretical scaffold for investigating petit apartheid. This is accomplished by an overview of sociological and legal theories that consider the existence and impact of informal, hidden processes on public processes. Each provides context and groundwork for understanding petit apartheid and outlining for a typology.

Informal Stages

Georges-Abeyie is not the first to comment upon the importance of evaluating the informal or hidden stages of social institutions. In *The Presentation of Self in Everyday Life,* Erving Goffman (1973) discusses the "back region." Also referred to as the "back stage," it is defined as a place "relative to a given performance, where the impression fostered by the performance is knowingly contradicted as a matter of course" (p. 112). What appears in the front region is presumed to be a statement of reality—the way things are. In fact, however, the front and back regions are inextricably linked, one informs the other. Goffman refers to this as "impression management" (p. 113). This analysis is valuable because it effectively demonstrates that what goes on behind the scenes is as important as what takes place in public view. Further, that people may have a vested interest in *not* disclosing the details of the back region.

Goffman's identification and analysis of the back stage is applicable to Georges-Abeyie's discussion of the informal stages of the criminal justice system. The back stage is where most racially-biased decisions are made (e.g., a police department policy that singles out minority motorists for vehicle stops). Because the back region does not constitute a formal stage (e.g., arrest), there is little official documentation of how and why decisions are made and whether race was a factor. In effect, there is little accountability for actions taken in the back region. Thus, racially-motivated decisions made in the back stage are easily presented as racially-neutral ones in the front region. It is also noted that not all back stages are out of view—some are simply not subject to official record-keeping or systematic scrutiny.

Charles Lawrence III (1987) offers a legal analysis that complements Goffman's back stage analysis. Lawrence assesses the covert, unconscious mechanisms that allow racism to perpetuate in the public sphere (e.g., government entities) (see also, Lopez 2000). Even when challenged as unconstitutional, these racialized practices often escape sanction. Courts, Lawrence says, do not "see," therefore, do not sanction racial bias that is not overt. To remedy this blind spot, he argues that another test should be applied: The "cultural meaning" test. This test would be used to determine whether a particular law or policy should be struck down as racially-biased. The cultural meaning test would provide courts with a broader, more accurate measure of how race influences decision making: "The test would evaluate governmental conduct to see if it conveys a symbolic message to which the culture attaches racial significance" (Lawrence 1987, 355-358).

Lawrence argues that such undercover legal work is required because society "no longer condones overt racist attitudes and behavior" (Ibid.). Consequently, true racial attitudes surface through the "collective use of actions, words or signs [which] represent shared but repressed attitudes" (Ibid.). By way of example, Lawrence highlights a case involving the construction of a wall which separated a Black and White community in Memphis, Tennessee [(*Memphis v. Greene* (1981)]. The lawsuit alleged that the wall was built to keep Blacks segregated from Whites, in violation of the Fourteenth Amendment. The U.S. Supreme Court held that because the city had no intent to be racially exclusionary, there was no constitutional violation. As Lawrence points out, had the Court applied the cultural meaning test, it would have considered a variety of factors, including the long history of Whites' need to physically separate themselves from Blacks, as a symbol of superiority (e.g., White flight). Thus Lawrence concludes, in evaluating the affect of race on legal and social policy, it is imperative to consider both historical and contemporary contexts.

As noted, Lawrence's analysis is directed at how courts might more fairly evaluate and redress racial discrimination by government entities. It is apparent, however, that *the court system itself* could reasonably be subjected to the cultural meaning test. That is, the same race discrimination that plagues government entities, also affects the criminal justice system in general and the courts in particular. The same unconscious racism that Lawrence seeks to expose through the cultural meaning test, permeates criminal justice system policies and practices.

Lawrence's theoretical analysis connects directly with Leon Higginbotham's legal assessment of how race affects courtroom practices. Higginbotham's work offers a nexus to the examination of race within the criminal justice system. His critique focuses on racialized courtroom practices:

> [I]nstances of courtroom racism act as signals, triggering and mobilizing those racist attitudes and stereotypes in the minds of all the courtroom participants, and possibly affecting the judgement and actions of the judge, jury and attorneys...Racist occurrences in the courts are particularly powerful symbols, acting to reinforce,

legitimate, and perpetuate racism *in the broader society* (1996, 129) (emphasis added).

Higginbotham cites numerous examples of overt and covert racial discrimination in the courtroom. This includes a catalog of racial statements and inferences made by judges, defense attorneys, prosecutors, and witnesses on the stand (Ibid. at 137-151).

Adding yet another step in the petit apartheid theoretical chain is the work of Donald Black (1989). In *Sociological Justice*, Black argues that the law operates as a quantitative variable. He posits that the amount of law brought to bear in a particular case (e.g., whether an arrest is made) the type of law applied in a particular case (e.g., decision to charge) and the ultimate sanction (e.g., sentence) is variable. How the law operates in a particular case depends upon a range of factors, including the social status of the parties, their legal representation, and their interaction with other courtroom actors (e.g., judge, witnesses, jurors). Race is one of the factors that directly affects case processing outcomes. Ultimately, Black concludes that across cases, the application of law is neither static nor predetermined. Rather, how the law operates is determined by "the sociology of the case" (pp. 4-8). That is, the interaction between legal and extra-legal variables, such as type of case, race, gender, and class of the offender and courtroom actors affect how cases are decided (see also Crenshaw 1993). Thus, general pronouncements about "how the law operates" are always false.

Together, the work of Goffman, Lawrence, Higginbotham, and Black establish a solid foundation for Georges-Abeyie's petit apartheid thesis. Each offers a distinct and compelling rationale for looking beyond "official" practices and measures of racial discrimination. Goffman posits that what takes place in the back region is not readily apparent to the outside world. What happens in this hidden, back arena, however, is directly linked to what is presented in the front stage. Further, Lawrence suggests that when legislative or political motives are not socially acceptable (e.g., racially discriminatory actions), attempts will be made to cover them up and sanitize them. Any racial animus which exists in the back stage (thus, Lawrence argues, throughout society) will not voluntarily be placed in public view (the front stage). Therefore, he concludes that intentional racial discrimination cannot be used as the test to measure the existence of racial discrimination.

Adding to Lawrence, Higginbotham provides numerous examples, which demonstrate how racial markers are used in the courtroom to perpetuate notions of Black inferiority. Further, Higginbotham observes that various courtroom actors (e.g., judges, attorneys) have attendant back stages. Each is affected and driven by larger, society-level representations of race. Higginbotham argues that courtrooms have racialized scripts that are not subject to adequate checks and balances. These race-based practices remain largely out of view and, as a result, continue unabated. Black's analysis allows for an assessment of how a confluence of case-specific factors—salient among them, race of the offender—predict that Black offenders will experience harsher treatment (than Whites) at each stage along the criminal justice process. The combined offerings of Goffman, Lawrence, Higginbotham, and Black illustrate how micro and macro-level forces intersect and work to reproduce the status quo.

As the above discussion indicates, petit apartheid practices within the justice system have three distinct, though interrelated features. First, these practices occur largely out of public view. Second, petit apartheid proliferates where criminal justice personnel have high levels of unchecked discretion. Third, these practices reflect and reinforce the racialized images of deviance that exist within society at large. The next section charts some of the locations and forms of petit apartheid.

Table 1—Preliminary Typology for Petit Apartheid

Forms of Petit Apartheid

CJUS System Continuum	Laws & Legislation	Policies (Formal & Informal)
Pre-Arrest	* Anti Gang Legislation (e.g., *Chicago v. Morales*)	* Racial Profiling (e.g., drug courier profiles motor vehicle stops)
		* Fetal Endangerment Policies
Charge Decision	————> * Prosecutorial Discretion * ————>	
	(e.g.,waive juveniles to adult court)	(e.g., when plea bargains will be accepted)
Sentencing	* Two Strikes & Three Strikes Legislation	* Differentials between White v. Blue-Collar crimes
	* Mandatory-Minimums (e.g., federal crack law)	

Outline of a Preliminary Typology

Table 1 outlines the broad strokes of a petit apartheid typology. The sketch identifies some of the legal and policy mechanisms that enable racial discrimination to proliferate within the justice system. These mechanisms (horizontal column), are examined at three points along the justice system continuum (vertical column). It is noted that these highlighted processes and forms of hidden bias are only one part of the problem. As discussed earlier, there are other mechanisms at work, which allow for differential group treatment. For example, when police communicate—verbally and non-verbally—with minorities in a disrespectful manner. That is, in a manner that sends a clear message of inferiority and subordination. Therefore, the stages and processes of petit apartheid outlined below should be considered *in addition to* those referenced above (see Introduction, Table 1).

Locations and Forms of Petit Apartheid

Each cell in Table 1 represents an insular and discrete example of petit apartheid. Each highlights a law or policy that has had a disparate impact on Blacks—a disparity that cannot be explained by disproportionate rates of Black offending. In the pre-arrest stage, the table provides two examples of ostensibly race-neutral laws that single out minorities for harsher treatment.

The anti-gang legislation, challenged in *Chicago v. Morales* (1999), illustrates how racial fears can act as the impetus for enacting legislation in areas with large numbers of minorities. This case involved a challenge to Chicago's Gang Congregation Ordinance. Under the law, a police officer who observed a "criminal street gang member loitering in any public place with one or more persons" could require them to disperse or be subject to an arrest. As written, the law allowed police to arrest gang and non-gang members. For example, a person waiting to hail a taxi or standing in a doorway to avoid the rain, could be stopped under the Chicago law. During the three years the law was in effect, the police issued over 89,000 dispersal orders and made more than 42,000 arrests. The majority of the people charged under the ordinance were Black and Hispanic. Opponents of the law argued that it allowed for arbitrary police enforcement and violated citizens' due process rights. The Supreme Court agreed and struck down the law as unconstitutional.

As Table 1 indicates, laws are but one manifestation of petit apartheid. Criminal justice policies are another form. In some instances, these policies are formal, written laws. In others, they are unspoken directives. Whether formal or informal, some criminal justice policies operate in a manner that allow law enforcement officials to disproportionately target minorities. The racial profiling of minority motorists (e.g., Driving While Black) is perhaps the most well-known example of this problem (see Russell 1999). Studies done in New Jersey and Maryland indicate that officers singled out Black motorists for traffic stops at rates far in excess of their rate of drug-related offending and rates of travel. As well, a Justice Department study of U.S. Customs found that Customs' officers were nine times more likely to stop, frisk, and x-ray Black women travelers than White women. Notably, Black women were less than half as likely to be found with contraband than White women (Government Accounting Office 2000, 2, 10).

"Fetal endangerment" refers to policies designed to identify and punish drug-addicted, pregnant women. South Carolina's application of these laws offers a textbook example of how racially-neutral laws can be applied in a racially-discriminatory manner. In 1989, the Medical University of South Carolina implemented a policy that allowed staff members to secretly test pregnant women for substance abuse. The non-consensual drug testing policy was designed to target pregnant women suspected of crack cocaine addiction.

The names of women who tested positive were given to the prosecutor's office. During the first year of the policy, with one exception, all of the women who were arrested and prosecuted by the Solicitor's office were Black women. Interestingly, the lone White woman charged under the policy was listed as having a "Negro boyfriend." Also noteworthy, the drug testing policy only applied to the Medical University, the only public hospital in Charleston, and the one hospital with a predominantly African American patient population. In June 2000, nine Black women and one White woman appealed their criminal cases to the U.S. Supreme Court. They argued that the Charleston policy amounted to an unreasonable search and seizure, in violation of the Fourth Amendment [*Ferguson v. Charleston* (2000), Paul-Emile 1999].

As the above two examples demonstrate, policies which allow law enforcement officers to use Blackness as an indicator of criminality (in the absence of empirical support), have the effect of *creating* Black criminality. This is particularly problematic at the pre-arrest stage. When racialized practices occur at the pre-arrest stage, they significantly increase the probability that Blacks will enter the criminal justice system.

As Table 1 demonstrates, petit apartheid practices continue well-beyond the pre-arrest stage. One example is legislation that gives prosecutors the sole authority to waive a juvenile over to adult court. On the surface, such legislation appears to be race-neutral. However, a look at how juvenile waivers are applied, suggests that race plays a role (e.g., Poe-Yamagata and Jones 2000, 12-13). Specifically, the research indicates that after controlling for offense type, minority youth are much more likely to be waived over to adult criminal court than White youth. This racial disparity continues through conviction and sentencing (Ibid. at 14-15). Placing the power to waive solely with the prosecutor increases the threat of racial disproportionality. An example of this is California's Proposition 21, which allows prosecutors to determine whether a youth shall be charged as an adult.

Beyond the charge decision, sentencing is another stage at which racial disparity is readily apparent. For example, Blacks are more likely to be charged under repeat offender laws—e.g., two and three-strikes laws. The racial impact of mandatory minimums is even more striking. More than 90 percent of those serving time for violating the federal crack law are Black or Hispanic. In 1999, 85 percent of the people sentenced were Black (4,391), 9 percent were Hispanic (463) and 5.4 percent were White (278) (United States Sentencing Commission 2000, 69).

The above is a preliminary offering of a petit apartheid typology. It is one step toward developing a schema for locations within the justice system wherein race-based decision making occurs. A fully-realized typology would include each stage of the justice system—e.g., arrest, pre-trial detention, plea, voir dire, opening and closing arguments, parole and post-incarceration. As well, it would include criminal justice system practices (as distinguished from policies) that allow race-based decision making to occur. Routine police use of excessive force against minority citizens (e.g., a particular police department) would be an example of this.

Conclusion

Georges-Abeyie's petit apartheid fits within earlier sociological and legal theories that examine hidden, below-the-surface behaviors. What makes Georges-Abeyie's contribution unique is his contention that there are back regions within the criminal justice system. His articulation of petit apartheid offers an alternative, preferable analysis of whether and how the criminal justice system operates to create racial disparity. Specifically, Georges-Abeyie identifies several locations along the justice system continuum where racialized practices pass for business as usual. These practices are oft-times invisible because they are not subject to official record-keeping and do not involve overt racial discrimination.

A cursory sketch of some of the processes that result in petit apartheid indicate that there are myriad locations and forms of race-based decision making. Future research should continue to explicate the typology, to include more forms of petit apartheid and how these forms course through the criminal justice system. For example, other loci for discretion-turned-discrimination include pre-trial detention, arrest, voir dire, opening and closing arguments and post-sentencing. Further, future work will need to consider the overall, societal impact of race-based practices within the justice system. As well, the impact of petit apartheid on specialized populations, e.g., young, Black men, must be assessed. That is, an analysis of the *cumulative* effects of petit apartheid practices on particular groups. To do otherwise, is to treat the criminal justice system's vise-grip hold on African Americans as a social fact rather than a social problem.

Cases Cited

Chicago v. Morales (1999) 527 U.S. 41.

Ferguson v. Charleston, No. 99-936 (2000) On Writ of Certiorari to the United States Court of Appeals for the Fourth Circuit, Brief for Petitioners, 1999 U.S. Briefs 936.

Memphis v. Greene (1981) 451 U.S. 100.

2

Walking the Beat Alone:
An African American Police Officer's
Perspective on Petit Apartheid

Jackie Campbell

On March 25, 1999, a police sergeant in a large metropolitan city, while working in a predominately African American section of the city, was shot at point blank range while on routine patrol in a high narcotics area. The offender was described as a male black teenager, 16 years of age, 5'8" and 140 pounds. Shortly thereafter, an intense manhunt ensued for the offender. Minutes after the description of the suspect was given, a call was received of a possible suspect aboard a bus, several blocks from the area of the shooting. Within minutes of the call, numerous police officers and the media responded to the scene of the incident. With cameras rolling, several police officers were filmed dragging young black males off the bus and throwing them to the pavement. These officers, unaware or unconcerned about the presence of the media, commenced to roughhouse numerous black males, some not even remotely matching the original description given of the wanted subject.

To some, the officers were within the scope of their power, trying desperately to solve a violent crime that happened to one of their own. To others, however, the conduct by the police depicted the type of treatment that the African American male has experienced on a daily basis for numerous years. This conduct is what Daniel Georges-Abeyie has referred to as petit apartheid. Was this a form of excessive force that African Americans claim to experience by agents of the criminal justice system on a daily basis? Or, was this proper police procedure? This essay will reflect upon my experiences as an African American female police officer and how I handled instances of petit apartheid both against minority citizens and against me.

According to Georges-Abeyie, when a question arises concerning whether or not there is discrimination in the criminal justice system the focus of analysis is usually on the formal, easily observed decision-making processes within the system. What is absent from this analysis, however, is the everyday insults, rough brutal treatment and unnecessary stops, questions and searches of blacks that usually go unreported and as such, the analysis omits data that would answer the question of whether there is discrimination in the criminal justice system. This treatment, termed "petit apartheid" by Georges-Abeyie, is often overlooked when studies are conducted to determine if the criminal justice system is racist because victims are often unwilling to report that the event ever happened. Since little empirical data exists to show that petit apartheid exists, many critics have concluded that there is no measurable differential treatment of minorities versus whites once they enter the criminal justice system. In my experience as a police officer, I found that quite often, instances of harassment and other improper police procedures were not reported by minorities because of the perception by minorities that the police officer was acting within the law. Thus, what Daniel Georges-Abeyie referred to as petit apartheid is often viewed as proper police procedure in many minority neighborhoods.

Early in my career, I observed that things that most citizens consider routine and non invasive, such as traffic stops, were almost always conducted differently when the violator was a minority. For example, it was likely that after conducting a vehicle stop in a predominately minority community, the driver was expected to immediately raise both hands in the air upon approach by a police officer. Initially, I thought this was just an isolated event but after witnessing this on numerous occasions, I learned from a veteran officer that this was protocol for stopping a vehicle in "high narcotic areas." I also began to realize that not only did the officer expect this of the violator, but that the violator considered this proper protocol for being pulled over for merely running a red light. Thus, this instance of petit apartheid became so normal that it became the rule to raise both hands in the air upon being approached by an officer rather than the exception.

According to Randall Kennedy in *Race, Crime, and the Law*, the question whether, or under what circumstances, police should be able to view and act upon race as a mark of increased risk of criminality frames a context in which the struggle between competing attitudes is tough. Whether the legal system ought to authorize people to take race into account in making calculations about criminal propensity is a vexing question.

In my experience, it became clear that the attitude of many police officers working within my district was that not only was it fair to use race as a proxy for dangerousness, it was an expected form of what I call "reasonable racial discrimination." Police officers thus believe that to attack the growing drug problem it was reasonable and rational to use a person's race as a signal for criminality. For example, often when a young male black was observed in an expensive car, it was customary for officers to assume that the driver was a drug dealer. After all, according to one veteran officer, how else could he afford to be driving a Lexus? When, however, a young white male was observed driving an expensive car, he was immediately labeled as a spoiled, rich, suburban kid cruising through the area. The importance in the distinction between these two individuals is that because the black male was labeled as a drug dealer, he was more often stopped, searched, and questioned, whereas the white male was more often stopped and warned about the danger of the neighborhood. Again, these instances of petit apartheid were expected norms of police/citizen interaction in minority neighborhoods. Thus, the citizens expected the police to stop them for driving expensive cars and the police expected the citizens not to question their use of reasonable racial discrimination to eradicate the drug element in the neighborhood.

Nowhere is petit apartheid more apparent in minority neighborhoods than in the enforcement of drug laws. Some have commented that urban police departments often focus on disadvantaged minority neighborhoods in combating the trade in illegal narcotics because it is easier to make arrests where social disorganization (the cornerstone of most of these communities) exists. In practice, however, police officers find it easier to make arrests for drug violations in minority communities because the Fourth Amendment to the United States Constitution means less in these communities than in other communities.

In my experience, police were often faced with the dichotomy of eradicating the drug problem in minority communities and staying within the parameters of the Fourth Amendment. Soon, however, it became apparent that ridding the community of drugs and staying within the realm of the Fourth Amendment, became difficult, if not almost impossible to do. Police officers, determined to answer the pleas of the community to erase the widespread drug problem in these areas, often resorted to whatever means necessary in order to get the job done. The results of this philosophy quite often resulted in warrantless searches of individuals, directly in opposition to the Fourth Amendment to the U.S. Constitution. As one veteran officer put it, "You do what you have to do to make the arrest and you worry about the probable cause later." The justification for these searches would always be the officer's good faith attempt to rid the depressed community of the drug element.

Many critics have questioned whether black practitioners in the criminal justice system have a positive impact on the treatment of minorities in the criminal justice system. In my experience, the race of a police officer often had little effect on how a minority suspect was treated primarily because of the immense pressure minority police officers faced in trying to be like the majority and also because most police officers often took an "us versus them" approach. It became apparent very quickly that if you sympathized with a suspect or if you exhibited concern about how a citizen was treated, especially in instances of apparent petit apartheid, you would be ostracized and considered an outcast. Thus, making a difference often meant walking the beat alone.

I came on the job as a police officer believing that I could make a difference. I was determined to do a good job, and in fact, I vowed that I would show my co-workers that it was possible to be a "working" police officer, while at the same time, staying within the parameters of the U.S. Constitution. A "working" police officer is a police officer with a high number of Part 1 Index Crime arrests and drug arrests. Where most police officers concentrate on answering calls for service on their beat, the "working" police officer, in addition to answering calls, actively seeks out dangerous felons and drug offenders. Because of the difficulty of getting good information about on-going crime, officers who are able to arrest subjects for drug offenses and violent crimes are considered to be the top officers and often have priority in receiving assignments to specialized units and coveted positions. This in part is a primary reason why officers resort to questionable measures when trying to apprehend suspected offenders.

In my quest to become a "working" police officer and avoid questionable measures to apprehend suspects, I decided to enroll in law school so that I would learn the requirements of the U.S. Constitution. After graduating from law school, I decided to police in one of the toughest areas of the city, known for high crime and poverty. I also decided that I would live in the same community so that I could really have a stake in the outcome of the area.

The first time I was confronted with opposition from other police officers was when I responded to a kidnap of a young black male. I responded to the job with two other white male police officers. Immediately, I sensed something was not quite right upon being dispatched to the job. Upon arrival, the complainant stated that two masked men entered her apartment, grabbed her teenage son, and forcibly threw him in the trunk of a car and sped off. While I was trying to gather more details about the crime, I noticed that the other police officers who responded with me were off in a corner laughing and discussing some matter, not even remotely related to the kidnapping job. When I questioned the officers about their cavalier attitude, I was told that this was probably not a real kidnapping but just a dope deal gone bad. I could not figure out how the officers had come to that conclusion, having done little or no investigation into the incident. When I informed the officers that this was in fact a crime and that they were not doing their job as police officers, I was told that if I thought it was a legitimate kidnapping, I could handle the job myself. As a result of questioning the officer's attitude I became labeled as a rebel and as such, along with others of similar position, subsequently ostracized by other police officers.

Because of fear and isolation, many officers will not take a stand against obvious instances of petit apartheid. Let me relate more personally. As a result of standing up to the officers who refused to handle the kidnapping, I suffered the consequences. For instance, I often responded to jobs without "back up," and had to work dangerous assignments alone. In one instance, after responding to an assignment of a robbery in progress and confronting an armed suspect, other officers interfered with my attempts to call for help by jamming my radio transmissions. I was forced to transfer to another district because of increased hostility and harassment from other police officers.

Although I suffered a few negative consequences as a result of refusing to engage in petit apartheid, I noticed that other officers no longer engaged in this practice when I came around. The fact that I confronted the officers about their discriminatory treatment thus prompted them to correct their behavior and to be more cognizant of the civil rights of citizens, at least while in my presence.

After leaving the district that I had worked for more than eight years, I decided to try policing in another area of the city. It was there that I finally saw the dichotomy that exists between policing in predominately minority communities and policing in middle class communities. Right away, I noticed that the officers talked to the citizens differently, approached the citizens differently, and responded to the jobs differently. While working with a veteran officer in this new district we conducted a vehicle stop of a white male subject. Upon approaching the car, I noticed that the driver did not automatically raise his hands in the air as the black males did in the district I had previously policed. I noticed that the officer responded to the driver in a courteous manner, informing him of the nature of the stop as well as asking permission of the driver to search him. This was something that I had never witnessed before in my career. Never had I witnessed an officer ask for permission to search a vehicle. It was just a given that the officer had a right to search the vehicle. The citizens in the previous district never questioned it and the officers never questioned it.

Officers working in minority communities are allowed to get away with these instances of petit apartheid primarily because it is an accepted norm in the police culture. To eradicate the problem, other officers must take a stand and alert those who engage in petit apartheid that it no longer is the norm and that it will not be tolerated. Another important reason that officers are able to continue these instances of petit apartheid is because of the widespread denial that petit apartheid does in fact exist. This denial thus helps to perpetuate the mistreatment of minorities by the police. Until an affirmation is made that there is in fact a difference in the treatment of minority citizens petit apartheid will continue to exist well into the 21st century.

The reality of the African American experience with the police is that differential treatment does exist in economically depressed areas of the city. Further, the lack of information that minorities have with regard to how to deal with this widespread problem helps to fuel the discriminatory practices of the police department. Quite often, the complaints of minorities have gone unnoticed and thus, uncorrected. This, however, can change if minorities were informed of the procedures that should be followed when allegations of police misconduct occur. Misinformation continues to be one of the primary factors that contribute to police misconduct. At one point, many minority citizens in the area in which I worked believed that it was against the law to carry more than $200 in currency. Although this may seem far-fetched and hard to believe, this myth and many others exist within these communities. The only way that petit apartheid can be erased from these communities is by first acknowledging that the problem exists and then by informing citizens of their constitutional rights and what to do in suspected instances of police misconduct. Finally, officers must take a stand against this practice, even if it means walking the beat alone.

3

The Presence and Effect of
Micro/Macro-aggressions and Petit Apartheid

Douglas E. Thompkins

I am certain that my family and I were victimized by acts of racism when I was a child, but the situation that stands out in my mind as my first encounter with racism occurred when I was eleven or twelve years old. I attended the 6th grade at a school that had been integrated by the construction of a nearby housing project. One of my classmates who happened to be white asked another classmate who happened to be Asian American and myself, the son of Natives and African Slaves, if we wanted to go fishing. There was a private lake not far away, where a person could pay to fish. My white classmate had gone there with his family and thought it would be fun if we all went there for the day. The few days leading up to our trip were filled with excitement as we made plans and prepared for the big event. The morning of the trip we met in the front of our school and began the five-mile walk to the lake. When we arrived at the lake tired from our journey, yet excited that we had made it, we walked up to the gate and were met by an older white gentleman. He looked at my Asian American classmate and me as though we had done something wrong, then turned to my white classmate and said, "you can come in but your 'nigger' friend and your 'chink' friend have to go home." We all stood there for a moment not certain of how to respond. My white classmate was placed in a position where he had to choose between walking through the gate and fishing or leaving with us, he chose to leave. As the three of us turned and began walking home we avoided eye contact with each other and walked in silence. The following Monday when we saw each other in school our relationship had changed. We did not know how to act towards each other and developed a pattern of avoiding one another.

I am not certain I fully understood the significance of what had taken place. Sure, I was conscious of the fact that I had just been denied the right or privilege of fishing because of my race, but the act was about more than my not being allowed to fish. I had been discriminated against because of my race, denied a right or privilege afforded others simply because of my race. We never talked about what had happened to us, but I have wondered how my two classmates came to terms with our experience and whether they have thought about that day in later years. I find that the experience has become more significant as I have grown older. On the one hand, this is because I am a student of the social sciences and I study issues of race, class, and gender. On the other hand, it is because I am confronted with acts of racism, or "micro and macro-aggression" on a regular basis.

Micro-aggression is a term used to describe racial assaults which are "subtle, stunning, often automatic and non-verbal exchanges which are 'put downs' of Blacks by [Whites]" (Russell 1998:138; Davis 1989). Examples of micro-aggression include a cab driver who refuses to pick up a Black passenger, a White person who enters a business office and assumes that the Black person she or he sees is a secretary or a janitor, or a White person who refuses to give directions to someone Black (Russell 1998). Macro-aggression is a term used to describe the attacks, insults, or pejorative statements made against Blacks by Whites. Macro-aggression differs from micro-aggression in that these acts of racism are not directed at a particular Black person, but at Blackness in general. Also, macro-aggression may be an action taken by a private individual or official authority (Russell 1998).

I used to get offended when a woman approaching me on the street grabs her partner's arm or changes the location of her purse to have a better grip on it. Or when I walk into a major department store to find myself being shadowed by security personnel. I used to get angry when I walk into a nice restaurant and the employees and patrons look at me as though I do not belong there or cannot afford the cost of a meal. It is as though my presence (man of color) reduces the level of exclusivity assigned the establishment and the status of the patrons who eat there.

I have developed different defense mechanisms that I use in an attempt to deter acts of micro and macro-aggression from taking place. When I walk into certain stores I take my money out of my pocket and hold it so people can see it, hoping they will not see me as a potential thief. When I see a woman approaching me on the street or walking in front of me, I cross to the other side because I do not want her to fear me, fear is a terrible emotion. When I go into certain communities I dress more conservatively than I normally do because I know many people have bought into socially constructed stereotypes concerning what is or is not part of the "gang uniform." I use these defense mechanisms to deter some of the insults I receive, but also, to shield myself from the emotions that arise in me in response to acts of micro-aggression that are directed towards me as an individual and/or acts of macro-aggression directed towards me because of my Blackness.

When a member of a law enforcement agency directs acts of racism towards me, the experience is more severe and there is the potential for me to suffer extreme levels of personal harm. It is suggested that the criminal justice system is no longer marked by intentional or widespread racial discrimination (DiIulio 1996; Wilbanks 1987), and that people of color are not adversely affected by acts of racial discrimination carried out by members of the criminal justice community (Tonry 1995). At the same time a growing body of research suggests that the informal stages of the criminal justice process must be included in any analysis of racial discrimination. Georges-Abeyie (1990) posits that discriminatory and discretionary actions of police officers during the "informal stages," such as pre-arrest, result in "petit-apartheid." Petit-apartheid consists of "...the everyday insults, rough or brutal treatment, and unnecessary stops, questions and searches of blacks; the lack of civility faced by black suspects/arrestees: the quality, clarity, and objectivity of the judges 'instructions' to the jury when a black arrestee is on trial; the acceptance of lesser standards of evidence in cases that result in the conviction of black arrestees, as well as numerous other punitively discretionary acts by law enforcement and correctional officers as well as jurist" (Georges-Abeyie 1990:12).

Petit apartheid as coined by Georges-Abeyie (1990), has been and continues to be very much a part of my life as a man of color in America. As a young man growing up on the South-side of Chicago my friends and I often faced acts of petit apartheid. It was common for us to be stopped by the police who would order us to get out of the car, demand that we empty our pockets and search the vehicle. We came to believe that these stops occurred most often when there were two or more men of color riding in one car. Our response was to ride alone in hope that we would not be stopped. Some times these stops could become brutal. The police would order us to lay face down on the ground while they searched our vehicle and talked to us in a very disrespectful manner. One police office who was known in the community as "gloves" because he wore black tight fitting leather gloves and liked to beat on people, was feared because he had a badge and a gun and acted more like a gangster than a police officer. There were times when after being pulled over by the police, one of the officers would say to the other, "I sure could use a few dollars," and the other officer would respond, "me too." This was a message to us that they wanted money in exchange for leaving us alone. I can remember being told: "You're one of those smart niggas, I hate smart niggas," and being asked, "Nigga don't you know I can kill you and nothing will happen to me?" On one occasion, this was done while a gun was pointed in my direction. I doubt that agents of the state act out this type of behavior in white communities?

During the fall semester of 2000 I traveled back and forth between the University of Iowa and the University of Illinois at Chicago on a regular basis. Driving east and west on Interstates 80 and 88, I began to notice men of color standing or sitting on the side of the highway with their hands often handcuffed behind their backs while a state trooper searched their vehicle. Once I became angry because a young man was sitting next to the rear of his vehicle on the side of the road closest to traffic. The state trooper had a dog with him who appeared agitated and was barking. Seeing this I thought of what might be going through the young man's mind. I spent the rest of the trip to Chicago pondering how I would deal with a situation like that. The young man had clearly been put in harm's way by being ordered to sit next to his car on the side of the road where traffic was flowing. I thought about what it must feel like to be sitting there with your hands handcuffed behind you and a police dog barking in your face, not to mention the traffic speeding by. I observed these types of incidents approximately six times over a period of four months. I must admit that I am now frightened by the possibility that I could end up sitting on the side of the highway while my vehicle is searched. Not because I broke the law, but because I am a man of color living in America and fit a particular profile.

I find it difficult to accept those arguments suggesting that people of color are not adversely affected by the racism that remains a part of the criminal justice system. If what they suggest is true, I am suffering from a severe case of paranoia. Petit apartheid is so much a part of life and the lives of millions of other Americans that we have all developed strategies and approaches for avoiding contact with agents of the state and for interacting with them if and when we are stopped. I refuse to be in a vehicle at night or in certain communities with more than one other male. When I get into my car I remove my hat and place it on the seat beside me because I know that my style of hat, worn the way I wear it, is part of the gang profile used by agents of the state across the country and if worn could trigger a police officer to stop me. During interactions with agents of the state I begin to use "sir" and "ma'am" when responding to their questions. I do this automatically without thinking about it. I hate what this suggests about me! I do not normally respond to people my age or younger using "sir" and "ma'am." I despise that part of myself which fears another human being because of what they represent. Fearing the police has the same effect on me as my fear of the Ku Klux Klan on the side of a dark deserted road in Mississippi in the 1960s. I do not fear the person inside the uniform, I fear the uniform and the power of the state that often sanctions the behavior of their agents, creating an environment within which I can be discriminated against, and even killed.

Petit apartheid, "racial discrimination at the pre-arrest stage of the criminal justice process," does occur and does adversely affect the lives of millions of people. This is not a new development. Relationships between agents of the state and minority communities have always been confrontational. The use of profiles and the criminalization of people of color began early in America's history. The slave codes passed in 1712, by the South Carolina Legislature provided for slave patrols to protect the rights of large plantation owners who controlled the state legislature. Slave patrols consisting of three men were charged with maintaining discipline, catching runaway slaves, preventing slave insurrections and enforcing laws against literacy. The slave patrols which were made up of working class white men, would invade slave quarters and terrorize blacks caught without passes after curfew (Lowe 2000). Policing, then, was first developed as a planter class strategy of race and class control. Police departments replaced slave patrols but the Black laws re-established the police practices of the slave codes (Center for Research on Criminal Justice 1977).

Today, profiles and ordinances such as the Chicago Gang Loitering Ordinance have similar effects on the lives of people of color because these practices and laws create an environment that allows for petit apartheid to take form and adversely affect the lives of people of color and women. Within certain inner city Chicago communities it is common for two or more men of color to be ordered to disperse. Between 1992 and 1995, agents of the state in Chicago issued over 89,000 reported orders to disperse and arrested over 42,000 people for disobeying their orders, most of which were Black or Latino. Nationally in 1995, 46.4% of persons arrested for vagrancy and 58.7% of persons arrested for suspicion in cities were Black although Blacks made up only 13% of city populations (Roberts 1999). The Chicago Gang Loitering Ordinance and similar State policies have the same affect on the lives of people of color as the Slave Codes and Black Laws of yesterday. They allow for the acting out of racist beliefs by members of law enforcement agencies that increase the level of unnecessary interaction between people of color and the police. These interactions lead to the "rough or brutal treatment and searches of blacks, increased levels of arrest, and discrimination during the pretrial, trial, and sentencing stages of the criminal justice process" (Georges-Abeyie 1990).

Formal discrimination may have been removed from official policies but discrimination still takes place at the informal stages of the criminal justice process. The way that we do race, class, and/or gender at particular moments in time dictates power relationships and often determines the outcome of social interactions. Our identity and the identity we assign others are a product of our history, environment, and culture. The way we treat those we encounter and allow them to treat us is determined by the identity we assign self and those we are interacting with at that particular moment in time. I suggest that minorities suffer discrimination at the pre-arrest stage of the criminal justice process because of the way street level agents *do* race, class, and/or gender. The evidence shows that Blacks and Latinos suffer the greatest levels of discrimination. Arrest rates associated with loitering ordinances and statistics addressing crack cocaine arrest and convictions, show that Blacks and Latinos are arrested and convicted at disproportionate rates, and that they are sentenced to prison for longer terms.

Legislative and judicial bodies which render decisions creating polices and laws allowing agents of the state to do race, class, and/or gender in ways that result in citizens suffering discrimination are partially responsible for the discriminatory behavior of their agents. Petit apartheid takes place because we live in a society where race, class, and/or gender continues to influence the way people interact with each other and because street level agents of the state are free to act out behavior influenced by their own beliefs and biases. My experiences with many White people are filled with examples of micro-and macro-aggression being directed at me as an individual and as a member of the Black race (Russell 1998, 138; Davis 1989). My encounters with the police and the encounters of other people of color with the police have led to many of us being treated unfairly, being injured, arrested, and discriminated against during the stages of the judicial process. Petit-apartheid describes these encounters and the affect of these interactions on us as Black people, both as individuals and as a group (Georges-Abeyie 1990). If we are to investigate whether racial discrimination continues to be part of the U.S. criminal justice process we have to include an examination of the informal stages because it is here that citizens first interact with members of the criminal justice system (police) and it is here that racial discrimination first takes place setting in motion a process tainted by hidden and unconscious racism if not blatant racism.

4

Round Up the Usual Suspects: Racial Profiling and the War on Drugs

Jeanette Covington

In recent years, there has been a good deal of controversy about the extent of racial discrimination in the criminal justice system. Those who argue that discrimination is rare claim that the United States has but one set of laws and those laws are enforced evenhandedly. They, then, focus on the formal decision making process in the criminal justice system and typically try to show that any bias in decision making is isolated rather than systematic. In order to bolster the notion that decisions based on racial bias are isolated and rare, they seek out evidence that indicates that the criminal justice system regularly and predictably enforces the law using only legitimate criteria. Hence, in this view, if a disproportionate number of blacks are caught up in the system, it simply indicates that a disproportionate number of blacks are involved in crime.

Daniel Georges-Abeyie (1989) takes issue with these claims by arguing that racial discrimination in the criminal justice system only appears to be isolated and rare due to the focus on the *formal* decision-making process. He suggests that a focus on the *informal* decision-making process would likely indicate that bias is a more routine and predictable part of the process. For him, a look at the informal decision-making process is important because it tends to indicate that the law is not enforced uniformly. Indeed, an examination of the informal decision-making process is most likely to turn up cases of petit apartheid practices or instances in which there are separate applications of the law based on race.

By way of example, he cites an incident that occurred in Philadelphia in 1988. In this case, bias on the part of the police figured in their response to a situation in which one Hispanic female and seven white females were raped in Philadelphia. These females described their assailant as a slender black male. Based on this vague description, the Philadelphia Police Department stopped and questioned 20 to 40 year old black males in Center City Philadelphia, who weighed from 120 to 160 pounds and were 5 feet

4 inches to 5 feet 10 inches tall. In short, a large number of black males were stopped and questioned, with advance recognition on the part of the police, that all but one of these males were innocent. It is not certain that they ever found the rapist.

It is incidents like these that cause Georges-Abeyie (1989) to question claims that the US has only one set of laws that are enforced uniformly without regard to race. The fact that these black males were stopped based on skin color and not their own criminal behavior indicates to him that many black males can be treated as suspects if a single one commits a crime. Moreover, like most petit apartheid practices, this roundup of black males was not a part of official agency policy. Rather it was part of the informal decision-making process. Hence the number of black males harassed, demeaned or humiliated by this dragnet did not become a part of official statistics. Since informal decisions like these typically remain hidden, it is difficult to determine just how much bias figures in criminal justice decision-making.

In 1988, the Philadelphia ACLU filed suit and convinced the police department to end this particular form of racial roundup. However, the practice of stopping numerous innocent blacks because of the alleged criminal behavior of a few is alive and well in the year 2000. While such petit apartheid policies continue to take many forms, perhaps the most pervasive example today is the practice of racial profiling on the highways (Harris 1999a, Russell 1998, Harris 1999, Cole 1999).

With racial profiling, black and Hispanic motorists are disproportionately stopped and searched on the highways (Harris 1999a). In the course of these stops and searches, numerous innocent minority motorists across the country have complained of treatment by the police that is variously described as rude, demeaning or humiliating.

In making these stops, the police typically use traffic violations as a pretext for apprehending certain motorists (Harris 1999b, Cole 1999). Using traffic violations as a pretext gives them wide latitude to make stops because most motorists invariably violate the traffic code in one way or another. The police can then pick and choose who they will stop (Goldberg 1999).

However, these stops do not reflect a simple concern about minor traffic violations. Rather the police use these stops as a pretext for investigating other crimes such as the transport of drugs, and many minority motorists have been stopped in this search for contraband. Indeed these highway stops have acquired their own name; namely, driving while black. Furthermore, those state troopers who admit that they single out black motorists typically argue that race is a legitimate criterion to use in deciding whom to stop and search because blacks are more likely to use, sell and carry drugs.

In this chapter, the issues surrounding the petit apartheid practice of racial profiling on the nation's highways are explored. The next section begins with a brief look at the anecdotal and statistical evidence that indicates that stopping and searching a large number of blacks is a routine and predictable part of the informal decision-making process for some state troopers. This is followed by a section that examines some troopers' claims that race is a legitimate criterion for deciding which motorists to stop and search. Those troopers who argue that targeting motorists by race is a legitimate practice typically justify these searches by claiming that blacks are more likely to use, sell and transport drugs than whites.

These claims are carefully scrutinized in a review of *objective* data on the extent of black involvement in drug crimes. In the course of this discussion, an effort is made to determine whether the objective data support this contention that blacks are more likely to use, sell and thereby carry drugs. A section in which the development of the practice of racial profiling is seen as the outgrowth of *subjective* factors rather than objective factors follows this. One subjective factor identified as crucial in the development of this policy is the late 1980s rise in public fears about minority drug use. A second subjective factor that has been used to justify the targeting of minority motorists is the drug courier profile. Both these factors are discussed in some detail.

Documenting Racial Profiling

There is a good deal of anecdotal evidence from African Americans and Hispanic motorists that they are singled out for stops and searches on the highways (Harris 1999a). Yet, such anecdotal data has typically been dismissed as the isolated experiences of angry, overly sensitive or disgruntled minorities. Still, there is some statistical evidence that seems to confirm these minority motorists' suspicions that they are being singled out for stops and searches.

A review of these studies using statistical data leads to several conclusions (Cole 1999, Leadership Conference on Civil Rights 2000, Lamberth 1996, Verniero and Zoubek 1999). First, it is clear that black and Hispanic motorists are no more likely to speed than whites so that they are not being targeted due to their traffic violations. Rather, race seems to be the pretext for these disproportionate stops and searches. Secondly, to the extent, that minority status is being used as a pretext to stop and search certain motorists for drugs, it is not a very good one. The fact that whites, who are searched, carry contraband in equal proportion to blacks and Hispanics, suggests that race does not affect the likelihood that motorists will carry drugs on the highways.

For example, in a study of traffic stops in Maryland, blacks made up 17.5 percent of motorists and an equal proportion of speeders. However, they made up 75 percent of those stopped and searched. Yet, despite the fact that blacks were more likely to be searched than whites, they were no more likely to be carrying contraband. The proportions carrying drugs were nearly identical as 28.4 percent of blacks and 28.8 percent of whites were found in possession of drugs (Cole 1999, Leadership Conference on Civil Rights 2000). Similar findings emerged in a New Jersey study where blacks made up 15 percent of motorists and 53 percent of those searched. An additional 24 percent of those searched were Hispanic and 21 percent were white (Verniero and Zoubek 1999). Yet 10.5 percent of the whites searched and 13.5 percent of the blacks searched were carrying drugs or weapons.

It is clear from these studies that the rate at which blacks are searched is not consistent with the rate at which they carry drugs. Hence, if traffic stops are to be used to search for drugs, then these studies suggest that the police should stop and search many more white motorists if they are interested in seizing more contraband.

Justifying Racial Profiling: Is Race a Legitimate Criterion?

In the face of such dramatic disproportions in the percentage of blacks stopped and searched, some state troopers have been known to openly admit that they single out blacks for stops and searches (Goldberg 1999, Cole 1999). For example, memos circulated among the Maryland state police urged troopers to be on the lookout for black males and black females who were believed to be carrying drugs (Goldberg 1999, Harris 1999b, Cole 1999). Further, former New Jersey State Police Superintendent Carl Williams stated that most of the illegal cocaine and marihuana business in the United States was conducted by minorities. He also claimed that the heroin traffic was mainly associated with Jamaicans (Harris 1999b, Donohue 1999a).

Many of those state troopers, who openly acknowledge that racial profiling occurs, go on to argue that they only stop and search more blacks because blacks are more likely to use, sell and carry drugs. In this view, singling out blacks based on race is a legitimate criterion because it greatly increases the chance that contraband will be found. Presumably, then, while discrimination exists, it is rational discrimination.

The notion that blacks should be targeted because they are more likely to carry drugs assumes that an accurate source of data exists on the prevalence of drug use and drug selling in the population. Presumably, then, state troopers might have been guided in their decision to single out blacks based on such data. As it turns out, data on arrests and imprisonment suggest that blacks are disproportionately involved in the use and sale of drugs. For example, 1998 arrest data indicate that blacks, who make up 12 percent of the population, account for 36.8 percent of those arrested for drug offenses nationwide (U.S. Department of Justice 1998). Hence, an uncritical interpretation of these data would suggest that targeting blacks on the highways would be the most efficient way to search for drugs.

Seemingly, the former head of the New Jersey State Police, Carl Williams, had these data in mind when he was asked about why so many African American motorists were stopped and searched in New Jersey. Pointing to 1997 arrest data for New Jersey alone, he noted that 50 percent of those arrested for drug offenses in the state were black and 13 percent were Hispanic. In other words, fully 63 percent of those involved in drug offenses by his estimation were minorities (Donohue 1999a). Because he regarded these arrest statistics as credible estimates of the prevalence of drug use and drug selling, he argued that singling out minorities for stops and searches was the most efficient way to use traffic stops to search for drugs.

However, most drug arrests are for possession and stopping lots of mere users on the highways will mean that only tiny amounts of contraband are likely to be seized. Prison statistics might be a better way of getting data on who is involved in drug selling as 70 percent of those in prison for drug offenses nationwide have been incarcerated for drug sales (Mumola 1998). New Jersey's prisons are no exception as fully 83 percent of those incarcerated for drug offenses in the state are locked up due to drug selling. Even more telling is the fact that blacks make up 81 percent of those locked up for drug offenses in New Jersey prisons (Human Rights Watch 2000). Hence, if former superintendent Williams had decided to consult prison statistics, he could seemingly have made an even stronger case for profiling black motorists.

However, using arrest and prison statistics to try to estimate levels of black and white involvement in drug use and selling is extremely unwise. Arrest statistics simply tell us what subset of users and sellers are actually apprehended. Hence, if the police were to conduct a number of crackdowns and sweeps in some of the state's predominantly white suburbs and rural communities, they would likely arrest a disproportionate number of whites.

Yet, as it turns out, a large number of police crackdowns and sweeps tend to be carried out in urban poor minority communities (Green 1996, Davis and Lurigio 1996, Weisbrud and Green 1994, Worden et al. 1994). Hence, arrest statistics and prison statistics simply tell us where the police crack down; they do not tell us anything about the true prevalence of drug offending for blacks, whites and Hispanics.

Indeed if arrest statistics are taken at face value, they provide what Harris (1999) defines as a self-fulfilling prophecy. Simply stated, because the police look for drug crimes in predominantly black neighborhoods, they disproportionately find drug crimes in these communities. By contrast, the drug crimes of whites are likely to be underrepresented in arrest and prison statistics because their neighborhoods are considerably less likely to be subjected to crackdowns and sweeps (Covington 1997, Tonry 1995).

The fact that the police are far more likely to look for drugs on the highways by stopping and searching a disproportionate number of black motorists only makes these lopsided arrest and prison statistics more questionable. In short, racial profiling on the roads in combination with a predominance of police crackdowns in minority neighborhoods together account for these misleading racially skewed statistics.

Yet, arrest and prison data on the racial distribution of drug crimes are not simply misleading because they are generated by crackdowns, sweeps and highway stops that target minorities, they are also questionable because they are at odds with other potentially more credible data.

Race and Drug Use in the National Surveys

Given the problems with arrest and prison statistics, it is somewhat surprising that state troopers have not consulted data on drug use from two well-known national self-report surveys. One survey, the National Household Survey on Drug Abuse (NHSDA) was initially conducted in 1972 and was administered every 2 to 3 years until 1991. After 1991, it was conducted annually. The NHSDA is a probability sample that covers the US civilian population aged 12 and older. Moreover, blacks and Hispanics have traditionally been sampled in large enough numbers in this survey to insure adequate representation (Office of Applied Statistics 1999).

The second national survey, Monitoring the Future, is a probability sample of students in public and private high schools across the country. This survey has been conducted annually since 1975 (Johnston et al. 1998).

In both surveys, respondents are asked to report on their use of a wide variety of illegal drugs and both surveys have tended to show that blacks are no more likely to use illicit drugs than whites (Covington 1997, Office of Applied Studies 1999, Wallace and Bachman 1991). Questions have been raised about the accuracy of these surveys as respondents are thought to underreport their drug use. In particular, there are questions as to whether black respondents are more likely to underreport than whites. However, when corrections are made for inconsistent responses, blacks are no more likely to report drug use than whites (Johnston and O'Malley 1997).

Of central importance in both these surveys is the fact that some effort is made to draw a random sample that accurately represents the black, Hispanic and white populations. This is in sharp contrast to arrest and prison statistics that tend to under-represent whites and overrepresent blacks because the latter are more likely to be apprehended in crackdowns, sweeps and highway stops. Since these national surveys rely on random samples that more accurately represent blacks, whites and Hispanics in the population, their figures on race differences can be seen as more credible than those drawn from arrest and prison statistics.

An examination of recent data from the 1998 National Household Survey on Drug Abuse indicates that 74.3 percent of all current users who have taken drugs in the past 30 days are white, 15.4 percent are black and 10.3 percent are Hispanic. Since the US population is 71.5 percent white, 12.2 percent black and 11.8 percent Hispanic, each of these major racial and ethnic groups uses drugs in rough proportion to their representation in the population.

While these figures indicate that blacks are no more likely to use drugs than whites, they say nothing about racial proportions in drug selling. However, a study of respondents in the household survey conducted between 1991 and 1993 indicates that, on average, 16 percent of blacks and 82 percent of whites (includes Hispanic and non-Hispanic whites) reported drug selling (Human Rights Watch 2000). In short, blacks also sell drugs in rough proportion to their representation in the population.

It is worth noting that these findings from survey data are consistent with some of the aforementioned data on searches. In other words, the fact that approximately 28 percent of blacks and whites searched in a Maryland study and 10.5 percent of whites and 13.5 percent of blacks searched in a New Jersey study were actually carrying drugs is consistent with survey data indicating that blacks and whites use and sell drugs in roughly equal proportions.

All of this suggests that there are no credible, objective data that would have led highway patrols to target blacks in the first place. After all, in the absence of any data, the police might be expected to stop and search motorists in rough proportion to their representation in the population. They would have no reason to target blacks. And, if they made use of estimates from the aforementioned survey data, these statistics would also suggest that no group be singled out for stops and searches. This would mean that a little more than 70 percent of those stopped and searched would be white, 12 percent would be black and 11 percent would be Hispanic. Yet, as research cited earlier indicates, highway stops are not based on the type of random search, that might occur in the absence of data nor are they based on credible, objective data such as that derived from the national surveys. So, if objective data do not account for how a policy like racial profiling came to be so pervasive, then other factors must be identified to explain how blacks came to be targeted on the nation's roads. There are at least two subjective factors that might account for racial profiling—namely drug scares and drug courier profiles. These factors will be examined in the next two sections.

Drug Scares and Racial Profiling

It is possible that a policy like racial profiling was not based on objective data at all. Instead this practice may have been shaped by more subjective factors like a rise in public concerns regarding the drug problem. Public concerns regarding drugs did indeed rise in the late 1980s. For example, in January 1985, only 1 percent of Americans believed that drugs were "the most important problem facing this country" (Reinarman and Levine 1997). Yet 4-1/2 years later in September 1989, a whopping 64 percent of Americans saw drugs as the most important problem. Initially this seems somewhat surprising, as illegal drug use in general was stable or declining.

This pattern of a late 1980s decline also characterized cocaine (Bachman et al. 1997). After a major epidemic in cocaine use in the 1970s and early 1980s, cocaine use declined substantially in the late 1980s. The only type of cocaine use that was increasing in the late 1980s was crack-cocaine use. Hence, the upsurge in public fears was not tied to the large cocaine epidemic of the late 1970s and early 1980s. Rather public fears were tied to a tiny outbreak in crack-cocaine use in the late 1980s that were largely associated with crack use in urban ghettos.

While the crack-cocaine outbreak in the late 1980s was quite small by comparison with the much larger boom in cocaine use of the late 1970s and early 1980s, it generated much more negative media attention. During the late 1980s media-frenzy, broadcast media showed documentaries detailing the crack problem in the urban ghetto and at least some of these documentaries enjoyed very high Nielsen ratings (Reinarman and Levine 1997). Print media, likewise, printed stories detailing the horrors of crack use in the ghettos with repeated tales about crack mothers, crack related turf wars and drive-by shootings. As these stories remarking on the wretchedness of ghetto life were popular with viewers and readers, there was something of a bandwagon effect (Reinarman and Levine 1997, Leiber et al. 1996). In other words, after one television network or one major newspaper described the miseries of crack use in the inner-city to the public, other networks and newspapers across the country began to entertain their audiences with similar stories about the ghetto crack crisis.

Interestingly enough, this media focus on drugs did not occur in response to the huge cocaine epidemic that occurred among affluent whites in the seventies and early eighties. The media waited to focus their attention on the much smaller ghetto crack problem. Hence, while the crack outbreak of the late 1980s was relatively small when compared to the earlier cocaine epidemic, there was a very real epidemic in media coverage of the crack "epidemic" in the ghetto. The rise in the public's fear of drugs that took place between 1985 and 1989 occurred largely in response to an explosion in sensationalized media accounts of the crack epidemic in the ghetto. Indeed, tales of pathological drug users in the ghetto continue to have some entertainment value as a series on this topic appears on cable television in the year 2000 (Scott 2000). One can only wonder if a cable series on the agonies endured by white drug addicts would be equally popular.

These media stories on crack focused solely on problem users in the ghetto who neglected their kids, killed their drug trafficking competitors or traded their bodies for crack. There were also numerous tales of Los Angeles based gangs who went from city to city spreading the crack menace, although many of these stories have subsequently been debunked (Klein et al. 1988, Meehan and O'Carroll 1992, Maxson 1995). Because these media accounts of crack use single-mindedly concentrated on ghetto crack users involved in pathological behaviors, they have been accused of routinizing caricature (Reinarman and Levine 1997). In other words, the media took worst case scenarios of inner-city drug users that were the exception and by simple repetition made then appear to be the rule. Hence, while these tales of ghetto pathologies sold newspapers and increased ratings, they grossly overstated the levels of problem use in the ghetto (Covington 1997).

With the significant rise in public fears regarding crack cocaine that accompanied this media frenzy, politicians reacted by competing to see who was the toughest on drugs. This led to the passage of the draconian Anti-Drug Abuse Acts of 1986 and 1988 that made penalties for the use and sale of crack much more severe than similar offenses involving powder cocaine (U.S. Sentencing Commission 1995, Belenko 1993, Reinarman and Levine 1997). This "get tough" posturing on the part of politicians was in their self-interest as it guaranteed them the support of their now fearful constituents. By contrast, any attempt to cite data suggesting that media reports of a crack epidemic were grossly exaggerated would have led to accusations that a politician was soft on drugs. Hence, drug legislation was passed with little reference to data. After all, to point to credible data on drugs would likely have meant a loss of votes.

Not only did politicians and the media convince the public that a dangerous epidemic was afoot, they also offered a solution to a now frightened and concerned public. Apparently, the solution to the drug problem was a renewed effort to wage a war on drugs. No mention was made of the fact that the war on drugs had already failed repeatedly (Holohan 1972, Bertram et al 1996, Wisotsky 1986).

At the federal level, this renewed effort to wage the drug war led to the establishment of a Drug Czar's office that promptly appropriated money to further traditional supply reduction efforts, such as stopping drugs from being smuggled into the country. At the local level, the police proceeded to conduct more drug crackdowns and sweeps in minority neighborhoods to root out the crack scourge (Kleiman and Smith 1990, Weisbrud and Green 1994, Green 1996, Davis and Lurigio 1996). And, for state police, efforts to turn back the crack epidemic meant stopping and searching a large number of black motorists for drug contraband. The New Jersey State Police were no different from their counterparts in other states as they too waged a drug war by stopping and searching minority motorists on the state's highways.

After years of complaints from black motorists on the turnpike (Covington 1991), the New Jersey Attorney General's Office issued a report in 1999 that admitted that racial profiling occurred (Verniero and Zoubek 1999). In the course of the report, some reference was made to the fact that minorities may have been singled out for stops and searches on New Jersey's roads as a result of efforts to fight the late 1980s war on drugs.

> The potential for the disparate treatment of minorities during routine traffic stops may be the product of an accumulation of circumstances that can contribute to the use of race or ethnically-based criteria by creating the unintended message that the best way to catch drug traffickers is to focus on minorities. To some extent, the [New Jersey] State Police as an organization may have been caught up in *the martial rhetoric of the "war on drugs,"* responding to the call to arms urged by *"the public, the Legislature and the Attorney General's Statewide Narcotics Action Plans of 1987 and 1993"* (Ibid.) (italics mine).

The notion that minorities were more likely to be involved in drug trafficking also found its way into training videos for the New Jersey State Police. New Jersey troopers were trained to believe that violent Jamaican gangs were primarily responsible for transporting drugs and that these violent gangs could easily disguise themselves as professional black males by sporting suits and short hair (Carter 1999, Kocieniewski 1999). Apparently, these training videos are no longer used, but they certainly would have taught troopers trained in this fashion to be suspicious of almost any black male motorists whether they were wearing gang colors or the more traditional garb sported by black professionals. This type of thinking would have virtually required a roundup of a broad cross-section of black motorists on the state highways.

Of course, New Jersey was not alone in encouraging such petit apartheid policies. After being fired, ex-trooper chief Carl Williams alluded to profiling at the federal level to raise questions about why he was being singled out for discipline. He noted that the federal Office of National Drug Control Policy reported that crack dealers in Trenton, New Jersey were mainly African-Americans while dealers in powder cocaine and marihuana were mostly Latino and Jamaican (Chivers 1999, Office of National Drug Control Policy 1998).

The problem with this type of profiling on both the state and federal levels is that it fails to allow for a huge hidden drug market that might never be picked up by police statistics. This hidden drug market might well include a number of white users and sellers. In fact, there is some ethnographic data that indicates that such hidden markets exist. For example, ethnographies conducted in rural America suggest that white farmers are involved in growing marihuana that can then be sold domestically (Clayton 1995, Weisheit 1992). Another ethnography discusses white traffickers involved in importing and selling vast quantities of cocaine in California towns in the 1970s during cocaine's boom years (Adler 1993). Yet few of the traffickers in Adler's study were arrested, in part, because the police in these small towns lacked the resources to investigate and crack down. What these examples indicate is that law enforcement may overlook many markets. Hence it is unwise to make any definitive statement about which racial or ethnic groups do or do not sell drugs based on arrest data.

All in all, the notion that racial profiling is based on rational discrimination seems dubious because no credible data exist to justify targeting minorities. What seems more likely is that racial profiling was based less on actual data than on police efforts to adapt to a sudden rise in public fears about a relatively small drug outbreak. Yet to develop a policy based on subjective criteria like public fears rather than real data hardly seems like the mark of a professional police force. Still, before dismissing racial profiling as an irrational response to a drug scare, it might be helpful to consider whether the police might be relying on yet another type of data, namely their own expertise. Indeed troopers often defend their stop and search patterns by alluding to this expertise that grows out of the cumulative knowledge of numerous officers who routinely stop and search motorists. In theory, such cumulative knowledge should reflect what troopers have learned over time about the types of clues that are likely to figure in a successful search for contraband. The next section examines the nature of police expertise in identifying drug couriers to see if this type of data might support a policy like racial profiling.

Drug Courier Profiles as Data

For many state troopers, too much has been made of statistical disparities in the number of minorities stopped and searched. For them, arguments that racially disproportionate stops reflect police bias rather than police expertise only indicate that minorities are second guessing police work without the benefit of enforcement experience and on-the-job training. For example, after the Maryland State police were sued for racial profiling, one disgruntled trooper remarked that the drug war was over and that the good guys (i.e., troopers) had lost and been cast as racists (Goldberg 1999). He went on to add that, "They're (the courts) going to let the NAACP tell us how to do traffic stops...they're going to let those people tell us how to run our department."

On its face, it seems reasonable to assume that the police should have acquired a great deal of experience in determining how to spot suspicious activities. And, in fact, over the years, both state and federal police agencies (for e.g., Drug Enforcement Administration, US Customs) have developed drug courier profiles that enable them to identify suspicious travelers who might be carrying contraband as they pass through airports, bus terminals or train stations (Cole 1999, US General Accounting Office 2000, Russell 1998). These drug courier profiles have also helped them to single out suspicious motorists on the nation's highways (Russell 1998, Cole 1999).

Drug courier profiles refer to a set of characteristics that the police use to target motorists or travelers as suspects. By rights, they ought to provide invaluable information to individual officers as they reflect the accumulated wisdom of federal and state enforcement agents who have successfully picked out guilty parties over the years. And, while race is a factor in many of these drug courier profiles, it is not the only factor. Indeed a whole host of traits can be used alone or in conjunction with race to identify a suspect that merits a search (Cole 1999, Russell 1998, Goldberg 1999). The police have been known to refer to these drug courier profiles when they are accused of racial profiling since these profiles allow them to argue that minority motorists are stopped because they have other nonracial characteristics that fit a drug courier profile and not for race alone.

It is possible to consult several types of sources to determine how enforcement agents at the federal and state levels identify nonracial characteristics that arouse their suspicions regarding motorists or travelers. Informal interviews with state troopers, who regularly stop and search motorists, constitute one way to gauge what they consider to be legitimate criteria for searching a motorist or traveler (Goldberg 1999). There are also more formal sources such as police manuals that list motorists' behaviors that make troopers suspicious or court testimony by officers seeking to justify their searches (Donohue 1999, Knowles et al. 1999; Cole 1999, Russell 1998). The following characteristics were gleaned from these sources.

Table 1—Indicators of Suspicious Activities

- minorities driving expensive cars
- minorities driving old cars
- when blacks and Hispanics drive in neighborhoods where they do not belong
- motorist is carrying religious paraphernalia to deflect suspicion
- motorist is driving leased vehicle
- motorist with air freshener in the car to confuse drug sniffing dogs
- young black women travelers with long nails and hair weaves, who carry Fendi bags
- motorist carrying maps from source cities where drugs originate
- motorist with only one key in the ignition
- signs that motorist has been driving long hours without making stops
- motorist does not look trooper in the eye
- high odometer mileage, especially on a late model car
- motorist is carrying too much luggage
- motorist is carrying too little luggage

Many of these characteristics will strike some as vague and poorly defined. For example, it is not entirely clear what it means for a style of car not to "match" the black guys in it or for blacks or Hispanics to be seen as suspect because they are driving in neighborhoods where they "don't belong."

Moreover, at least some of these supposedly suspicious behaviors are likely to be regarded as highly ambiguous. For example, a motorist driving a leased vehicle could be a drug dealer who has rented a car to transport contraband or more likely an innocent motorist driving between cities. Or motorists might put air freshener in their cars to thwart a drug sniffing dog or simply because they like the scent. In short, most of these clues so strongly suggest a number of totally innocent motives that they offer little support for troopers' claims that they bolster their chances of finding contraband.

Indeed Cole (1999) found many of the characteristics that police dub suspicious to be so unconvincing that he described drug courier profiles as a "scattershot hodgepodge of traits and characteristics so expansive that [they justify] stopping anybody and everybody."

The traits listed are indeed expansive enough to give troopers broad discretion to stop almost anyone. Indeed because these indicators are so inclusive as to make almost everyone suspicious, they practically guarantee a number of law abiding people will be stopped needlessly. In fact, the only indicator of suspicion that eliminates a broad swath of the population is race, simply because it eliminates so many white motorists. This might lead some to urge the courts to reject all of these indicators because they are so sweeping in their definition of what constitutes suspicious behavior. In this view, drug courier profiles are little more than tools to provide law enforcement cover for thinly veiled efforts to search whomever they like.

Moreover, on the rare occasions when the traits in drug courier profiles have been tested, they have not worked very well. This is evidenced by the case of US Customs agents who were trying to spot drug couriers bringing drugs into the country at the nation's airports. Initially, they assumed that African-American female travelers were more likely than white American females to be carrying contraband (US General Accounting Office 2000). Hence, consistent with this profile, Customs agents subjected African-American females to nine times as many intrusive searches using x-ray exams as white females. Yet, an analysis of these searches indicates that white females were actually almost 2 times more likely to carry drugs than black females subjected to x-ray exams (US General Accounting Office 2000). In short, the rate at which black females were x-rayed was clearly not consistent with the rate at which they carried contraband.

That drug courier profiles can lead to glaring errors such as these is not all that surprising. After all, very little was required to justify using race as evidence of suspicious behavior. Instead of credible data, these profiles were developed in response to a drug scare that appealed to longstanding mainstream fears and hatreds of a "dangerous class" of people. They were then subsequently legitimized when hunches, intuitions and prejudgments on the part of the police were elevated to the level of police expertise.

The fact that African-Americans can be searched based on their skin color rather than probable cause or reasonable suspicion means that suspicion no longer attaches to the individual but to a whole race of people (Harris 1999). It is unfortunate that so little has been required to justify violating the Fourth Amendment rights of a whole race of people.

Summary and Conclusions

This chapter began with some acknowledgement of the fact that racial profiling on the highways is not the only type of petit apartheid practice that results in racial roundups. As recently as 1992, the police in Oneonta, New York tried to stop every young black man in town for questioning about a robbery. The police initiated their dragnet by obtaining a list of the black male students on the local college campus and then proceeded to question 78 of them. Using a rather vague description that indicated that the robbery suspect was a young black male who might have a cut on his hand, the police ultimately rounded up 200 black males for questioning in this town with a total of 500 black residents (Newman 1999). Blacks can also be rounded up and subjected to a "stop and frisk" for running at the sight of a police officer (Greenhouse 2000). In short, "running while black" is also sufficient grounds for the police to treat African-Americans as suspects in areas known for narcotics trafficking (read black ghettos). And "standing while black" has also been deemed suspicious activity as young African-American males were arrested in Chicago between 1992 and 1995 for loitering in any one place with no apparent purpose in the presence of a suspected gang member. The Chicago police could arrest young black males engaged in this crime of "standing" if they refused to disperse (Greenhouse 1999, Harris 1999). The Supreme Court eventually declared this particular type of roundup unconstitutional. However, the practice of stopping, questioning and even searching a large number of innocent blacks for the crimes of a few continues.

As these examples indicate, these racial dragnets are pervasive and easily justified as a necessary tool in waging a war against drugs or a war against crime. In this chapter, the notion that rounding up black motorists for highway searches is a useful tool in waging the war on drugs has come in for some scrutiny. There is reason to doubt that racial profiling furthers drug control efforts because there are no credible, objective data that suggest that blacks should have been targeted in the first place. Rather, blacks seem to have been transformed into the "usual suspects" in this case due to a late 1980s drug scare. The police reacted to these newly aroused public fears over drug use in the ghetto by cracking down on black communities, black travelers and black motorists. They then justified their actions by piecing together a drug courier profile. Unfortunately, these drug courier profiles have turned out to be vague, ambiguous and in some cases inaccurate.

Unlike many of the other types of racial roundups, both citizen complaints and statistical evidence have documented the widespread practice of racial profiling on the highways. Hence the extent of this aspect of informal police decision-making has been subjected to more scrutiny than other petit apartheid police practices. The results are simply startling and have forced the police to justify their discriminatory stops and searches by pointing to drug courier profiles.

The fact that the Fourth Amendment rights of African Americans can so easily be violated based on these vague, ambiguous and often inaccurate drug courier profiles is cause for alarm. Instead of searches based on probable cause or reasonable suspicion, the bar has been lowered so a whole race of people can be searched based on the hunches, biases and prejudgments of state and federal police. Moreover, the fact that dragnets can be initiated against these despised minorities based on longstanding fears rather than objective evidence is disheartening although hardly surprising. Perhaps, these petit apartheid practices will end when they are more carefully monitored and when the police are held accountable for these drag-nets. But, any serious campaign to end these discriminatory practices will also have to raise public skepticism about law enforcement rhetoric that suggests that these racial roundups are somehow effective tools in waging a war against crime and drugs.

5

Out of Place: Petit Apartheid and the Police

Sandra Bass

The American system of apartheid—a world in which there were separate schools, separate water fountains, and separate lunch counters for African Americans—is still a fresh wound on the American body politic. Despite the demise of de jure racial discrimination, informal discretionary decisions continue to perpetuate the discriminatory effects associated with the system of American apartheid. In the criminal justice system, this is perhaps most publicly apparent in low-level police discretionary decision-making.

Police discretionary decisions are affected by a range of factors, yet the impact of racial discrimination and residential segregation on the development of policing and police behavior is rarely explored. Placing this issue within a historical context demonstrates how state supported racial discrimination and segregation deeply affected the organizing ethos and practices of American policing. Further, even though the formal structures that created American apartheid have been dismantled, public policies and police discretionary behavior continues to perpetuate an apartheid-like relationship between minorities and the police. Georges-Abeyie has referred to the minutia of discretionary decisions made by criminal justice practitioners that adversely affect racial minorities as "petit apartheid discrimination" (Georges-Abeyie 1990). After a brief discussion of the impact of historical traditions on policing, this chapter will discuss the contemporary expressions of petit apartheid in policing.

Policing Race, Policing Space—A Brief History

Protecting spatial sovereignty is the primary function of the state. We most often think of this in its external dimension, that is the state's role in preserving and protecting national boundaries by mounting a military and if necessary going to war. Spatial sovereignty also has an internal dimen-

43

sion. This refers to the ability of the state to "exercise regularized control of its subject population" within its sovereign territories (Herbert 1997). In other words, on the domestic front, governments have an interest in "ordering," controlling, and sanctioning the actions and behaviors of it's citizenry. This is particularly true when these behaviors take place in public spaces. The police are the primary agents responsible for performing this fundamental governmental function

The regulating and policing of public spaces, however, has been deeply affected by our history of racial subordination and segregation. For the better part of our history race has been a central determinate in how public spaces were constructed and in the regulation of behavior in public spaces. Federal, state, and local governments as well as private actors engaged in a range of discriminatory practices in order to create and then preserve racial discrimination and segregation. Even though ethnic spatial segmentation has deep historical roots in America, when we speak of enforced racial segregation we refer specifically to the experiences of African Americans.[1] Segregation was a central tool for keeping African Americans in their "place" whether that be defined as a specific part of the city or a lower status in society at large.

Race and space have been important factors in social and public policy and thus they have also had a significant impact on the development of policing in America. Race as a means of defining space and regulating behavior in public spaces and thus, as an organizing element in police work, reaches back to the earliest days of policing. Although informal policing mechanisms began in the colonial period the emergence of a semi-formal, organized policing force can be traced back to slavery (Williams and Murphy 1990, Reichel 1999). Slave patrols were vested with virtually unlimited coercive authority in their charge to monitor the movement of slaves as well as track down runaways.

With the end of slavery, southern whites were faced with new economic and social control dilemmas. An important legal tool for ensuring the continued domination of the white population was the passage of broadly defined vagrancy and loitering statutes that came to be known as the Black Codes. Mississippi and South Carolina became the first states to pass such legislation near the end of 1865. African-Americans were prohibited from engaging in a broad range of "disorderly offenses" such as using insulting gestures or language, engaging in malicious mischief, preaching the Gospel without a license, or taking on employment other than farmer or servant with out paying an annual tax (Williams and Murphy 1990). Those who violated the codes were subject to a variety of punishments ranging from fines, to serving on chain gangs, to involuntary labor on a plantation. The Black Codes essentially created a set of legal tools for monitoring and regulating the black population and ensuring the continued subordination of black labor to white economic power.

As the Black Codes came under legal attack, southern states began aggressively pursuing radical racial segregation as a means of ensuring white supremacy and black subordination. One of the great ironies of history is that a practice which became synonymous with the South actually began in the North. In the South, the proliferation of Jim Crow grew out of economic crisis, political opportunism, and racial fears (Woodward 1968). Jim Crow advanced rapidly as a means of resolving multiple problems. The intent of Jim Crow was to continually reaffirm and remind the black population of their lesser status or "place" in the larger society. Essentially African Americans lived in a police state in which virtually every aspect of shared public life was proscribed. Formal police organizations under this system were responsible for upholding both the formal and informal social order. The formal police in the segregated South represented both the repressive civil order of the South as well as the ideology of white supremacy overall. "He stands not only for civic order as defined by formal laws and regulations, but also for white supremacy and a whole set of social customs associated with the concept" (Myrdal 1944, 535).

Black migration from the South to the North surged after both World War I and II. Northern industrial cities such as New York, Detroit, and Chicago were primary sites for black migration. As the black population grew so did the tools and means for containing newly arrived blacks into burgeoning ghettos. Federal policies played a significant role in encouraging white flight to the suburbs and restricting African Americans to specific inner city neighborhoods.[2]

Local political leaders, real estate agents and developers, and community-based neighborhood preservationists used a variety of tactics to discourage blacks from moving to white neighborhoods. Although less widely recognized, racial discrimination and social control through residential racial segregation was also a factor in the development of western cities with appreciable black populations (Bunch 1990). As Sugrue notes, in the post-war city, "blackness and whiteness assumed a spatial definition" (Sugrue 1996, 9). The inability to live beyond the boundaries of the ghettos and to move freely within the city without fear of police harassment severely restricted the civil liberties of African-Americans. In 1963, one black minister in Detroit argued that the system of racial segregation in which those with "the desire and ability to move without the right to move" amounted to "refined slavery" (quoted in Sugrue 1996, 258).

This brief historical review is critical for understanding the contemporary context of American policing with regard to race. First, legalized discrimination has had a profound impact on the police. As the primary agents of domestic law enforcement, the police were responsible for upholding and enforcing discriminatory laws. Further, the record shows that racial minorities have historically been viewed as objects of law enforcement and social control rather than citizens entitled to civil protections. The centrality of race in the formation and organizing ethos of the police is critical for understanding the impact of race on contemporary policing policies and practices.

Second, federal, state, and local governments had an active role in creating and preserving the apartheid system. Policy decisions at all levels of government continue to be a central factor in perpetuating the differential treatment and outcomes of minorities who come in contact with the police. Third, this history illustrates the close relationship between racial subordination and the control of public spaces. Spatial segregation provided a means for differential delivery and distribution of public goods and services to black communities. As Gunnar Myrdal noted, residential segregation created "an artificial city... that permits any prejudice on the part of public officials to be freely vented on Negroes without hurting whites" (Myrdal 1944, 618). In other words, residential segregation provided a means by which wholly different standards of public service could be delivered without adversely affecting the majority white community. As the police are essentially a spatially deployed public service, race and space are central to the historical development of the police. Policing in the segregated zones has historically been qualitatively different from that in predominately white neighborhoods. Further, residential segregation created cognitive boundaries that defined those "places" that were relegated to racial minorities and those that were not. African-Americans and other minorities who ventured outside of their neighborhoods were often subject to police harassment for having the temerity to circulate "out of their place."

Finally, even though *de jure* racial discrimination has ended we have seen in recent years the resurgence of police policies and practices that continue to perpetuate a quasi-apartheid like relationship between racial minorities and the police. The intrusive police practices associated with the "war on drugs," a subject discussed at length in another chapter in this volume, are a clear example of this relationship. However, the growing popularity of "quality of life" policies illustrate the continued saliency of race and space in determining policing policies and practices.

Petit Apartheid Policing and the "Quality of Life"

In 1982, Wilson and Kelling became the standard bearers of the current resurgence in order maintenance or "quality of life" policing with the publication of their article, "Broken Windows" (Wilson and Kelling 1982). Based primarily on research conducted in Newark, New Jersey, Wilson and

Kelling argued that quality of life environmental factors such as graffiti, trash, litter-filled lots, and unrepaired broken windows, as well as low-level disorderly behavior such as prostitutes gathering on corners, aggressive panhandlers, and the inebriated were critical indicators of community disorganization and disregard. Left untended, these neighborhood conditions signaled to the criminal element a community lacking the necessary social organization to manage its own public life, and thus a prime target for victimization. Wilson and Kelling advocate assertive police order maintenance actions as a means by which police could help re-establish and/or strengthen community behavioral norms. Although Wilson and Kelling consider the potential for inappropriate and undesirable police behavior with the adoption of these practices, they fail to state any remedies for these potential problems (Wilson and Kelling, 1982).

Since the publication of "Broken Windows," order maintenance or "quality of life" policing has been at the forefront of policing. In his bid for the New York mayor's office, Rudy Guiliani made quality of life a central point in his campaign. Upon winning the office, Guiliani tapped former Transit Chief William Bratton as Police Commissioner, who soon introduced sweeping changes to the NYPD. Bratton reorganized the NYPD and introduced a computer-driven, problem-oriented internal accountability system known as COMPSTAT. Bratton also questioned the effectiveness of the community policing practices instituted under former mayor David Dinkins and Police Commissioner Lee Brown. Bratton, instead, refocused the police on "quality of life" offenses and advocated assertive and prominent police actions that has come to be termed zero-tolerance policing (ZTP).

Although it's unclear whether ZTP is true to Wilson and Kelling's original conception of Broken Windows policing, it is true that Broken Windows theory has been the legitimizing premise behind the implementation of ZTP. Bratton instructed officers to crackdown on squeegee men, petty drug dealers, graffiti taggers, prostitutes and other quality of life offenders. Officers were encouraged and expected to assertively stop and question "suspicious persons" as a means of discovering violations as well as obtaining information on other criminal activities. In order to empower patrol officers to address neighborhood drug problems, Bratton lifted a 20-year-old corruption-reduction reform that banned patrol officers from engaging in drug arrests. He also created the Street Crime Units (SCU), plain clothes officers who are deployed specifically to apprehend serious offenders.

The ramifications of these new policing directives were felt most deeply by the city's minority and immigrant population. The number of minorities stopped and frisked rose precipitously with the introduction of zero tolerance policing. African Americans constitute only 25.6 percent of New

York city's population, yet they comprised just over 50 percent of all persons stopped. 33 percent of persons stopped were Hispanic, even though Hispanics comprise only 25 percent of the population. [Office of the New York State Attorney General (ONSAG) 2000.] Nearly two-thirds of stops conducted by the SCU were of African Americans. Moreover, blacks and Hispanics were at a greater risk of being stopped in neighborhoods in which they constituted a distinct minority. In precincts in which African Americans and Hispanics constituted less than 10 percent of the population, they constituted 30 percent and 23.4 percent of the stops respectively. Relatively few of these stops resulted in arrest. New York police stopped 9.5 African Americans, 8.8 Hispanics, and 7.9 whites for every one arrest. The disparity is even greater for the SCU who stopped 16.3 African Americans, 14.5 Hispanics, and 9.6 whites for every one arrest. This disparity holds even after controlling for crime rates by race (ONSAG 2000).

Advocates of ZTP often point to the falling crime rate in New York as evidence of its effectiveness. Any analysis of the drop in crime in New York however, must weigh the range of other factors that affect crime rates, such as economic health, demographic factors, and changes in the drug economy. Further, recent research questions both the causal connection between disorder and crime and the suggestion that NYPD tactics are responsible for the crime drop. Harcourt reexamined the original data from the Newark and Houston fear reduction studies and found that the connection between disorder and future crime was weaker than had been previously reported (Harcourt 1998). A longitudinal study of 66 Baltimore neighborhoods found that neighborhood structural factors had a greater impact on future crime than changes in the level of "incivilities" (Taylor 1999). Other cities, notably San Diego, have experienced drops in crime similar in magnitude to New York without adopting aggressive quality of life policing (Greene 1999).

Despite evidence that questions the connection between crime and disorder, many cities, citing the dramatic drops in crime in New York, have rushed to duplicate the NYPD model as the latest weapon against crime. The architects of the New York plan have built lucrative careers consulting cities on how to implement ZTP. In Cleveland, police officers have increased the number of stops conducted sixfold in recent years (Innes 1999). The victory of Baltimore City Council member Martin O'Malley in the city's recent mayoral race has been largely attributed to his campaigning on a "zero tolerance" on crime platform (Paik 1999). Baltimore Police chief Tom Frazier resigned his post rather than implement a zero tolerance plan designed by New York consultants (Rosen 2000).

ZTP practices have also had a deleterious affect on the relationship between minorities and the police in New York. Since the implementation of ZTP complaints against the police rose 41 percent with many of these complaints coming from people of color (Greene 1999). However, the deaths of Amadou Diallo and Patrick Dorismond best underscore the tragic consequences of unrestrained police aggression. In February of 1999 Diallo, a Guinean immigrant, was gunned down in the foyer of his Brooklyn apartment building by SCU officers who mistook Diallo's wallet for a gun. In the subsequent criminal trial none of the four officers were held criminally responsible for his death. Patrick Dorismond, a security guard and the son of a Haitian official was killed by NYPD officers running a marijuana sting when he reacted negatively to an officer's aggressive overtures to procure marijuana from him. The officers who killed Dorismond were part of a new narcotics enforcement team named "Operation Condor." Officers working Operation Condor are required to have five narcotics arrests per shift or risk the wrath of their supervisors, a directive that likely encourages officers to engage in unnecessary stops and arrests.

Police practices to address gang violence illustrate another area in which petit apartheid and zero tolerance practices flourish. Gang violence has become a critical concern for law enforcement. Addressing gang violence and crime challenges fundamental principles of our legal system. While the criminal law is structured to contend with the acts of individuals, crimes committed by gang members are attributed to their group membership. Unless law enforcement agencies can find ways to tie specific individuals to a crime, they often can not prosecute individuals they believe are tangentially involved in criminal activity. In some instances, law enforcement believes that gang violence and crime persist because individuals who are on the periphery of the gang protect them or enable their behavior. Further, there is a belief that preventing gang-related crimes requires the adoption of measures which destabilize gang structure and organization.

The police have developed several tools to address gang crimes. One common law enforcement tactic is the use of gang profiles. Much like drug courier profiles, gang profiles seek to delineate the distinguishing characteristics of gang members. Gang profiles focus on physical attributes and associational affiliations as indicators of gang membership. Like drug courier profiles however, gang profiles are often a poor means for identifying gang members. Rather than a compilation of actual behaviors, gang profiles often focus on clothing, territory, identification by an informant, and affiliations. These are particularly poor measures given the widespread adoption of "gang" clothing (e.g. baggy pants, scarves, shaved heads) in popular culture and the often fluid nature of social interactions among young people.

The means of identifying gang members are also racially biased and have resulted in the exponential growth of young men of color being named as gang members. Nearly half of young black men in Los Angeles

County have been defined as gang members or gang associates. In Orange County, California there are reportedly 13,609 identified gang members, approximately 75 percent of who are Latinos, while the remaining are predominantly Asian. In Denver, Colorado two of every three young black men in the city are on the gang list. Even though white gangs are known to exist and to engage in violent and deviant acts, white gangs are often not viewed as a problem (Kim 1996, 275). "Community opinion of white gangs,...tends to be less critical than that of gangs comprised of different races" (Kim 1996, 271). Hence the definition of what constitutes a criminal gang is itself racial biased and contributes to the disproportionate number of minorities defined as gang members.

Despite the imprecision of gang profiles as a means of identifying criminal gang members, law enforcement agencies conduct broad "sweeps" in inner city neighborhoods using these loose criteria to identify "gang members." In many respects these sweeps illustrate en masse the practice of indiscriminate "stopping and questioning." Further, many jurisdictions use this information to compile lists of "known" gang members to be used by law enforcement and officers of the court. Some agencies keep photographic logs of suspected gang members. Some states, such as California, have developed computerized statewide databases consists of the names of known gang members. Once an individual has been defined as a gang member, they are subject to any enhanced penalties that might be in effect for gang-related offenses and may have their movements monitored by law enforcement. The accuracy of these databases is contestable. As mentioned, gang profiles are a notoriously imprecise means for identifying gang members. Secondly, although these databases are supposed to be purged every two years, it is unclear whether this is done on a timely basis. In some instances, the names of deceased "gang members" have been found on a gang list years after their death. Finally, there are no provisions for purging the names of gang members who have left the gang life. Essentially once some one is entered into the database it is unclear how and when they will have their names removed.

Relying primarily on vague and overly broad stereotypes to identify gang members has resulted in the wholesale labeling of young men of color as gang members in some jurisdictions. In this respect, gang profiling, much like other discriminatory practices, continues to perpetuate discriminatory discretionary police practices that disproportionately affect young men of color. Much like the Black Codes of previous eras, in some jurisdictions gang profiling has developed into a system for "keeping tabs" on virtually an entire generation.

Quality of life policing has also been introduced as a means of abating gang violence. Relying primarily on public nuisance laws, several jurisdictions have filed civil injunctions that severely restrict the behavior of "known" gang members in public spaces. Police and prosecutors compile extensive dossiers documenting the activities of suspected gang members and their associates and collect depositions from officers and community members documenting the nuisance behavior of individuals. This documentation is then used to civilly enjoin specified individuals from engaging in certain behaviors in specific neighborhoods. The number of enjoined individuals can range from 10 to over 100. The enjoined behaviors are typically quite extensive and cover a range of activities including loitering in public, being seen in public with two or more known gang members, trespassing on private property without written consent of the owner, disorderly conduct, wearing "gang" clothing, violating curfews, littering, blocking free passage of streets and parks, and noise. Approximately 30 gang injunctions have been or are in the process of being filed, most of which are in California. For the most part, developing case law has supported the constitutionality of the injunctions. (*People ex rel Gallo v. Acuna* 1997; *In re Englebrecht* 1998; *Iraheta v. Superior Court of L.A. County* 1999).

Gang civil injunctions effectively bar the young men named in the injunctions from appearing in public spaces in their neighborhoods. The potential for police abusing this extension of police discretionary power is far reaching. Officers may stop individuals indiscriminately to verify whether they are covered under the injunction agreement. As injunctions establish probable cause, enjoined individuals may be stopped at any time, regardless of whether their present behavior suggests reasonably suspicious behavior, to verify whether they are in compliance with the restrictions imposed by the injunction. Essentially gang injunctions give police *carte blanche* to engage in pretextual stops of suspected gang members in specific neighborhoods.

The dangers of using civil law in lieu of criminal prosecution are substantial. For one, due process protections are attached to criminal not civil proceedings. Enjoined individuals have no right to counsel and must provide their own legal representation. Further, the standards of evidence are substantially lower in civil cases. This has meant that prosecutors can obtain injunctive sanctions against individuals they could not convict in criminal proceedings.

One author compared the broad reach of anti-gang civil injunctions to the vague vagrancy statutes that were part and parcel of the Black Codes (Stewart 1998). However in looking at broken windows and zero tolerance policing policies and practices collectively, it can be fairly said that the potential for police abuse of discretionary power can be extended to this entire genre of police behavior.

Everything Old Is New Again

The policies and practices associated with zero tolerance policing suggest that what has evolved since the demise of de jure apartheid is a system of *de facto* racial discrimination driven by low-level discretionary decisions. This system perpetuates one of the fundamental aims of American apartheid by restricting the access and mobility of African Americans in public spaces for fear of police harassment. Many African Americans particularly fear being stopped and harassed by police when they venture beyond the borders of the black community. This fear appears to be borne out by the New York data which demonstrates that people of color are more likely to be stopped in white neighborhoods. This likely deters blacks from frequenting "white" neighborhoods. Indeed, if African Americans believe venturing into these neighborhoods invites unwanted police attention and thus avoid these areas, the system of petit apartheid is rendered virtually invisible and hence much more potent and effective.

Discrimination as a result of these practices is perhaps even more difficult to address because in many instances the practices are perceived as racially neutral. Because they are race neutral on their face the burden of proof falls on the victim to prove racial bias and discrimination. Given that low-level discretionary behavior are often out of the purview of the public, they are difficult to document.

Even in those instances in which racially disparate outcomes can be empirically established, the argument is often made that this is due to disparate offending rates and not discriminatory practices. This same circuitous logic was used in the South to defend Jim Crow, and in the north to support segregation (Woodward 1968; Sugrue 1996). In both of these instances the system of racial subordination which created the limited opportunity structure for African Americans was defended by pointing to the diminished achievements of African Americans as proof of their lesser status. With regard to the criminal justice system, the system of racially biased policies and practices that have resulted in disproportionate arrests and incarceration rates is defended by pointing to the very outcomes it has helped to create as proof of high levels of black criminality.

Affecting change in this area of police work can be accomplished however. Two decades ago community policing was more likely to be discussed at a conference for criminologists than the halls of city government. Yet today, community policing has emerged as the new paradigm for policing. The emergence of community policing as the preferred model of policing was not an accident. Rather, the shift to community policing was a product of "forced change" compelled by actors both internal and external to the police department (Zhao 1996). Meaningful efforts to eliminate racially biased policies and practices in other areas of police work would require a similar marshalling and coordinating of internal and external forces.

Endnotes

1. As Massey and Denton (1993, 2) note, "no group in the history of the United States has ever experienced the sustained high levels of residential segregation imposed on blacks."
2. For example, Massey and Denton discuss at length the impact of federal highway and FHA policy on encouraging racial segregation.

Cases Cited

In re Englebrecht, (1998) 67 Cal.App. 4th 486.
Iraheta v. Superior Court of L.A. County, (1999) 70 Cal. App. 4th 1500.
People ex rel. Gallo v. Acuna, (1997) 14 Cal. 4th 1090; 929 P.2d 596.

6

Trying to Make Us a Parking Lot: Petit Apartheid, Cultural Space, and the Public Negotiation of Ethnicity

Jeff Ferrell

Introduction

A host of contemporary controversies revolve around seemingly benign notions of urban redevelopment, enhanced public safety, and restored public order. Submerged in these controversies, though, is a dangerous and often unnoticed dynamic, a dynamic that Georges-Abeyie (1990a, 1990b) characterizes in terms of "petit apartheid." In Georges-Abeyie's formulation, petit apartheid incorporates both the criminal justice system's everyday, person-to-person discrimination against Blacks and other ethnic minorities, and also the patterns of racial segregation and public space allocation that structure such discrimination. And as this chapter will demonstrate, it is precisely this petit apartheid—this convergence of social control, the partitioning and segregation of public space, and everyday ethnic discrimination—that undergirds any number of key contemporary controversies. This convergence in fact shapes the political and economic frameworks of these controversies, as city officials and corporate developers work to reinvent and market new images of the city, to create urban "consumption spaces" (Zukin 1997, 227, 240) that symbolize safety and status, and to exclude from these spaces those ethnic identities that would intrude on their symbolic value. It drives new techniques of regulation and enforcement that emerge in and around these spaces—techniques that involve everyday petit apartheid, the everyday policing of public ethnicity and public perception. And it animates the subcultural dynamics of those labeled as criminal threats to these new arrangements; through such subcultural dynamics, they transform their criminalized identities into symbolic displays of defiance and resistance, and construct alternative ethnicities designed to escape new forms of petit apartheid.

Petit Apartheid and Cultural Space

Georges-Abeyie's (1990a, 12) powerful notion of "petit apartheid" specifically references the criminal justice system's range of "punitively discriminatory, discretionary acts"—including "everyday insults, rough or brutal treatment, and unnecessary stops, questions, and searches"—that constitute day-to-day discrimination against Blacks and other ethnic minorities. In light of this pervasive pattern of everyday injustice, Georges-Abeyie calls for "a criminological and criminal justice theory which is grounded in the experiential reality of non-whites," and which is "cognizant of the effect of site and situational factors" (1990b, 32) in crime, crime control, and crime victimization. Similarly, Russell (1998, 138-139) notes the day-to-day persistence of racial affronts to Blacks—affronts that take the form of both subtle, interactional "microaggressions" communicating distrust or disrespect, and broader "macroaggressions" undertaken "by a private individual or official authority" as an attack on "Blackness in general."

Significantly, Georges-Abeyie's apartheid metaphor denotes a system of day-to-day, situational discrimination that is at the same time spatial in nature—that is, intertwined with the allocation and control of public space. Just as apartheid in South Africa hinged not only on individual insults and brutality, but on spatial partitioning and large-scale ethnic relocation, contemporary petit apartheid in the United States and other countries incorporates the politics of space as well. Georges-Abeyie's notion of petit apartheid in this sense suggests that patterns of ethnic discrimination and of intra-ethnic and inter-ethnic criminality emerge not as free-floating phenomena, but in the context of what he calls expanding "residential spatial segregation." In addition, the concept highlights the "specific ecological zones of the alleged ghetto, slum-ghetto, or non-ghetto" that form the locus of discriminatory policing, and the broader salience of complex and changing "spatial dynamics" (1990a, 12-13).

Emerging perspectives in cultural and postmodern geography (for example Merrifield and Swyngedouw 1997, Rotenberg and McDonogh 1993, Soja 1989) support Georges-Abeyie's notion that any analysis of contemporary ethnic discrimination must be attentive to spatial and experiential dynamics, and to the encoding of discriminatory power relations in public space. Further, these perspectives point to the contested symbolic meaning of spatial arrangements, and to the ways in which these arrangements function to enforce existing intersections of power and inequality. In his analysis of street politics and street sensibilities, for example, Keith (1997, 139) argues that, through "the return to spatiality" in social theory, we can "reconnect economy and culture"; to this we might add crime and crime control, and contested constructions of ethnicity and public identity, as well.

In developing this key spatial dimension of petit apartheid, a similar spatial framework that has emerged within the field of cultural criminology (Ferrell and Sanders 1995, Ferrell 1999a, Ferrell and Websdale 1999) can also be of use. This framework is embodied in the concept of "cultural space" (Ferrell 1997, 1998, 2001). The notion of "cultural space" suggests that public spaces and city sectors—parks, streets and street corners, shopping districts, residential enclaves—function not only as utilitarian arrangements, but as deep repositories of meaning for those who own them, occupy them, or move though them. This meaning is in turn encoded and contested in the realms of image and perception, such that the occupation of these areas is always as much symbolic as physical, the presence of particular populations confirmed as much through stylized presentations of self as through simple census counts. Thus, various constellations of cultural space—the restored storefronts and gated communities of the affluent, the street corners of gang members and gutter punks, the back alleys of graffiti writers and the homeless—incorporate, along with issues of urban development and public safety, other issues essential to defining self and society. These cultural spaces mark the changing boundaries of private property and public propriety; shape the emerging image of the city and its residents; and drive the contested remapping of ethnic identity and public meaning.

Because these cultural spaces are meaningful, because they matter so profoundly in the construction of identity and perception, because they are worth fighting for, they emerge as essential contemporary zones of conflict, control, and resistance. Conflicts over cultural space incorporate not only the emerging political economy of the city, but new forms of politics, criminalization, and legal control. It is not by accident that cultural space controversies are so often publicly presented in the language of social problems and social safety, so often publicly encased in the vocabulary of crime and criminal threat; and it is not surprising that many of the most controversial new forms of social and legal control, and most spectacular forms of public resistance, have developed within and around these conflicts. Emerging institutions, evolving patterns of production and consumption, become at the same time domains for new forms of crime and criminalization, control and resistance. In the present case, then, an inquiry into contemporary public controversies becomes, inevitably, an inquiry into the interconnections between crime and crime control, politics, cultural space—and the construction, display, and erasure of ethnic identity.

And it is here, in this tangle of cultural, spatial, and interactional dynamics, that we begin to see a key linkage between contemporary cultural space battles, the public negotiation of ethnic identity, and the everyday spatial practices of petit apartheid: As new cultural spaces are carved out by city planners and corporate developers, they serve to segregate city life along new lines of spatial exclusion and petit apartheid, and to organize new forms of everyday discrimination, new patterns of microaggression and macroaggression, against ethnic minorities and others deemed foreign to these spaces. As the following discussions will show, it is in this context, and in the interest of enforcing and maintaining these new spatial arrangements, that new indignities and new aggressions emerge. Yet it is also in this spatial context that new forms of resistance and new images of ethnic identity are invented in counterpoint, and that new configurations of social justice can be imagined.

Case Studies in Petit Apartheid, Cultural Space, and Ethnic Identity

Across the wide range of contemporary public space controversies, essential categories of social life—class affiliation and privilege, gender, age, ethnicity—are consistently at issue. Critical Mass bicycle activists, for example, organize mass bicycle rides that confront not only the privileged position of the automobile in urban areas, but the parallel public subordination of women; as Caycee, a Women's Critical Mass activist says, "The first time I went to Critical Mass what struck me was that it reminded me of a Take Back the Night march.... by yourself, singly, you're powerless. You're subject to violence...death...aggression and harassment....And that's what makes it so powerful, that you feel that you're reclaiming the space, that by yourself is not yours" (Ferrell 1999b). In San Francisco's Mission District, the Mission Yuppie Eradication Project similarly battles the increasing gentrification of the neighborhood and displacement of its ethnic minority and lower income residents. With street fliers and posters written in English and Spanish, and calling for the vandalizing of yuppie automobiles and the destruction of high-end bars and restaurants, the Project has gotten the attention of well-to-do neighborhood newcomers and police alike. In fact, in a raid on the apartment of one of the Project's alleged instigators, police confiscate a framed picture of Malcolm X, and some 70 books "related to anarchism, communism, or revolution" (Gurnon 1999, A26). And, as the Eradication Project's bilingual fliers and Malcolm X photos suggest, issues of ethnicity pervade this and other public conflicts. For instance, increasingly popular youth curfews—designed to regulate the public spaces and times that young people can occupy in them, and in the words of one critic, to "make the town look like it doesn't have problems" (in Beck 1995, 53)—also target poor and ethnic minority kids disproportionately (Cox 1998; Daza 1996).

Three contemporary public controversies perhaps reveal most dramatically these threads of contested ethnic identity that run through cultural space conflicts. Specifically, they highlight the ongoing public construction of ethnicity and ethnic identity. At the same time, though, they highlight the economic, legal, and political forces that would erase these ethnicities from public spaces and public view—forces that in this process of erasure also spawn new forms of everyday aggression and petit apartheid.

Street Cruisers and Lowriders

In Hispanic and Mexican-American communities, the customizing of automobiles into stylized "lowriders," and the ritualized "cruising" of these customized cars along streets and boulevards, has existed for decades as a constructive alternative to gang membership, a significant leisure-time activity—"a Chicano alternative to Disneyland" (Rodriguez in Bright 1995, 99)—and a source of shared cultural pride. The cars themselves, and the murals that are painted on their hoods and door panels, embody symbols of ethnic heritage, and reference real and imagined ethnic identities. The ritual of collective street cruising, while certainly a source of self-made entertainment and pleasure, also incorporates a distinct sense of ethnic heritage and honor; the Phoenix-based Techniques Car Club, for example, not only cruises the streets on weekend nights, but escorts marchers celebrating events such as the birthday of Cesar Chavez, and accompanies neighborhood girls on their way to church for *quinceanera* rituals (Barker 1996, B4). Perhaps most importantly, as Bright (1995, 90-91) notes, lowriders and street cruising open up for young Hispanic and Mexican-American men and women opportunities for "public display and cultural pride," creating as they do a "mobile canvas for cultural representation" and "alternative cultural space" that transcends patterns of urban ethnic segregation and the usual "restrictions on the spatial mobility of racially marked men."

Despite cruising's affirmative cultural significance and essential role in constructing public ethnic identity—or perhaps because of these factors—legal and political power has increasingly been marshaled to remove cruising, and its potent ethnic symbolism, from public view. In 1979, Los Angeles County sheriffs cordoned off East L.A.'s Whittier Boulevard—the primary place "where La Raza, the people, came together to have a good time in cars" (Bright 1995, 99)—and made 400 arrests, effectively closing Whittier to subsequent cruising. More recently, Denver police have utilized street barricades, ticketing, arrests, and an ordinance regulating car stereo volume to push cruising off West 38th Avenue as it cuts through the traditionally Hispanic neighborhoods of north Denver (Ferrell 1996, 193). In Phoenix—where the local newspaper describes cruising as "a slow-moving parade of noise, litter, vandalism and violence" (Konig 1997, B1) and "neighborhood activists" proclaim their desire to have the avenues "wiped clean of cruising" (Fiscus and Kossan 1996, A1)—the City Council and police have designated "no-cruising zones," and enforced these through barricading, increased traffic fines, and aggressive enforcement of trespass and curfew ordinances. In addition, police have moved to "seal off" South Phoenix neighborhoods, and to ban "mostly Hispanic," non-resident teenager cruisers from them. In a revealing commentary on ethnicity and public identity, a City Councilman defended the plan by arguing that ethnicity "will not be the single factor to keep people out of the community" (in Kossan 1996, B2)—only the major factor. In response, local car clubs staged a mobile and public protest, the Cruisers Against Violence Caravan and March.

In a classic example of petit apartheid, then, the legal and political crackdown on cruising has spawned a plethora of everyday indignities and discriminatory acts—barricades, traffic stops, tickets, fines, arrests, no-cruising zones—aimed at dismantling the ethnically rich cultural spaces that cruisers create. And, significantly, the postscript to these legal and political maneuvers against cruising is a spatial one as well. In the years following the erasure of cruising from the streets of north Denver, the neighborhoods there have continued to see skyrocketing housing prices, a steady influx of middle class Anglo homeowners eager to live near Denver's revitalized downtown, and thus the steady flushing out of north Denver's largely working class, Hispanic population from these newly upscale areas. And in Phoenix, the local paper features a front-page article— "South Phoenix Undergoing Rebirth" (Kelly 1999, A1, A6)—that pictures an Anglo homeowner in front of his newly built home. Touting the area's proximity to Phoenix's redeveloped downtown, and the positive effects of the Baseline Area Business Plan—approved by the City Council, interestingly enough, in the same period of 1996 that it was developing a very different plan for street cruisers—the article proudly notes that the area has become "a Mecca of real estate development, a rapidly expanding area that's beginning to erase the stigma of crime, drugs, and prostitution south Phoenix has carried for years."

Hip Hop Graffiti

Like street cruising in Hispanic and Mexican-American communities, hip hop graffiti developed in Black communities some two decades ago as a street-level alternative to gang membership and gang conflict, and as a repository of alternative ethnic identity and stylish pleasure. Emerging along with rap music and break dancing as part of the larger, homegrown hip hop subculture, hip hop graffiti tags and murals ("pieces") remade the public spaces in which they were written. Early on, hip hop graffiti writers put their images in motion by painting them on the sides of subway trains; converted abandoned abutments and alley walls into colorful "walls of fame;" and gained subcultural status from tagging and piecing prolifically enough so as to "go citywide." More recently, writers have developed the practice of "tagging the heavens"—tagging at the highest possible location on buildings, freeway signs, and billboards—and have begun to "go nationwide" by tagging and piecing on freight trains (Ferrell 1998, 1996, 1995; Phillips 1999; Walsh 1996). In these ways, hip hop graffiti writers have continued to expand the cultural spaces that their graffiti invents.

In addition, hip hop graffiti has emerged as a public affirmation of ethnic communities, and as political critique. Hip hop graffiti writers are increasingly commissioned to paint colorful street memorials to community members killed by police or gang violence (Cooper and Sciorra 1994), and to execute public service and public health murals (Ferrell 1995). They also paint street-smart political commentary, as in Spon's mural questioning the N.Y.P.D.'s high-powered weaponry (in Cooper and Sciorra 1994, 72-73), and Voodoo's wall poem making fun of Denver's aggressively anti-graffiti mayor (in Ferrell 1996, 106).

Not surprisingly, these everyday images of alternative ethnicity have generated in response nationally-coordinated anti-graffiti campaigns designed to systematically erase them from public view. Funded by a mix of tax dollars and corporate donations, the campaigns incorporate features ranging from increased civil and criminal fines and longer jail sentences to the street-level use of infrared video cameras, night vision goggles, helicopter patrols, citizen surveillance teams, and sting operations (Ferrell 1995). Despite hip hop graffiti's origins as a street-level alternative to gang conflict and identity, and despite its rapid spread among Anglo and suburban kids in recent years, the campaigns also promote racialized panic over hip hop graffiti, continually and mistakenly essentializing it as a marker of ethnic gang violence and ethnic threat to public safety.

And in this context, the campaigns not only produce harsher legal punishments for graffiti writers, but spawn informal public attacks on them, producing a dangerous mix of microaggression and macroaggression. In Denver, for example, three men, "pumped up and emotional" from attending an anti-graffiti meeting, assault two teenagers they believe (mistakenly) to be graffiti writers, telling one of them "I'm gonna get a thousand bucks [reward] for your ass" (in Ferrell 1996, 128). In Southern California, anti-graffiti vigilantes take their aggression a step further, as an off-duty sheriff's deputy fires his service revolver into a group of taggers (Sandoval 1997), and a citizen shoots two kids he finds painting under a bridge, killing one, and referring to both as "skinhead Mexicans" (O'Neill 1995, B8).

As with street cruising, though, attacks on hip hop graffiti and its practitioners are driven by the racialized politics of urban economic development, by emerging spatial patterns of petit apartheid, as much as by the hostility of individual racists. With remarkable prescience, Denver hip hop graffiti writer Z13 anticipated the coming redevelopment of Denver's downtown LoDo district in explaining the erasure of Denver's original graffiti "wall of fame" in the early 1990s: "That wall along the creek there— of course, the reason there's so much interest in that is because they're redeveloping that whole area.... Back when we did the wall of fame it was... before they started working in that area, so it was still okay. But then once they started doing some work out there, all that had to go" (in Ferrell 1996, 105).

Gangs, Loitering, and Gang Injunctions

As Hagedorn (1990) and others have noted, ethnic street gangs engage in a variety of everyday activities, most of which go unnoticed when such gangs are conceptualized and accounted for only in terms of crime and criminal justice. While these gangs do, to varying degrees, engage in criminal and violent activities, they also construct shared styles and rituals that promote a larger sense of collective identity and expanded cultural meaning. Through dramatic sartorial styles and street monikers, through codes of street imagery and honor, gangs create a collective, stylized presence that undergirds their symbolic occupation of public space (Ferrell 1997). For many ethnic gangs, this occupation becomes also a symbolic defense of historical space and ethnic heritage, with gang styles and gang graffiti encoding the boundaries of neighborhood and community (Sanchez-Tranquilino 1995).

While purporting to address issues of gang violence and criminality, a host of recent legal and political initiatives launched against ethnic street gangs in fact aim directly at this symbolic occupation and defense of public space, and in so doing attempt to remove gangs, both symbolically and physically, from the cultural spaces they create. Legal definitions of gangs and gang identification checklists increasingly reference not activities, but public images; the Arizona Criminal Code (13-105; *Arizona Criminal and Traffic Law Manual* 1994, 26), for example, defines street gang members by their "paraphernalia," "tattoos," "clothing or colors," and other "indicia of street gang membership." Based on such identifiers, "known" street gang members encounter an astounding range of public legal controls. As Rodriguez (1994, M2) reports, Immigration and Naturalization

Service officials detain and deport Hispanic and Latino/a kids "simply because they were caught dressed like 'gang-bangers' and without proper identification." In Chicago, tens of thousands are arrested under a 1992 ordinance that allows police to arrest any "suspected" gang member who fails to disperse when found "loitering in any public place...with no apparent purpose." And though the Supreme Court struck down this law in a 1999 ruling, the Supreme Court justices stress "that with a little tinkering, gang loitering could be attacked legally" (Savage 1999, 50).

Such gang identification checklists, paired with official databases cataloguing "known" and "suspected" gang members, spin off other forms of petit apartheid, other everyday microaggressions and macroaggressions as well, from unwarranted police stops and illegal photographing of minority youth to banishment of "suspects" from particular buildings and housing areas (Siegal 1997). The most wide-ranging legal attack on gangs' public presence, though—and most potent breeding ground for petit apartheid and everyday discrimination—has come in the form of civil injunctions against gangs. Approved by the California Supreme Court in 1997, and utilized in California and other states, such injunctions prohibit "known" or alleged gang members from such public activities as: climbing fences; talking to people in passing cars; carrying glass bottles, marbles, or screwdrivers (Mowatt 1997, A1); "standing within ten feet of an open beer can" (Lait 1999, B2); and "'standing, sitting, walking, driving, gathering, or *appearing anywhere in public view*' with any other defendant or gang member" (Werdegar 1999, 18, emphasis added). In addition, such injunctions impose curfews for juveniles and adults alike (Rabin 1998, B3), and "give the police probable cause to stop and search members named in the court order at any time" (*The New York Times* 1999, 27). In Cicero, Illinois, such injunctions are utilized by town officials in their effort "to evict all gang members, including minors and people with no criminal records, from the town's borders" (Lait 1999, B2). In Phoenix, a neighborhood "activist" supports such gang injunctions by arguing that "this concept of rights for them has got to go away. The concept of rights for the good folks has to be protected" (in Fiscus 1998, A1); or, as California Supreme Court Justice Janice Rogers Brown writes in the 1997 majority opinion, "Liberty unrestrained is an invitation to anarchy" (in Jacobius 1997, 34).

The consequences of this logic have been revealed most vividly in Los Angeles. In the city's Rampart Division—described by the *Los Angeles Times* as having "one of Southern California's heaviest concentrations of transient and disaffected immigrants" (Lopez and Connell 1999, A21), most from Mexico and Central America—members of L.A.P.D.'s elite CRASH (Community Resources Against Street Hoodlums) unit have instituted aggressive anti-gang street policing, and have in addition provided court testimony essential to gaining broad anti-gang injunctions. An unfolding and ever-expanding scandal in the Rampart Division, however, has now not only uncovered pervasive police misconduct against alleged gang members—including false arrests, beatings, and shootings—but has linked this misconduct directly to the development of the injunctions themselves. Almost half the alleged gang members named in a major injunction, for example, were accused by officers now caught up in the scandal. In one instance, a CRASH officer fired for allegedly beating an ex-gang member provided a key overview of gang activities that led to the injunction against the gang (Lopez and Connell 1999a, 1999b). In another, "some of the most persuasive police testimony used by prosecutors to obtain a sweeping anti-gang injunction" was based on a "chilling portrayal" (Connell and Lopez 1999, A1; see Lelyveld 1999) of a gang member's armed attack on two police officers. In fact, the investigation now reveals, the unarmed gang member was handcuffed by the officers, shot, framed with a planted rifle, and subsequently sentenced to 23 years in prison. Released after serving 2½ years, he remains confined to a wheel chair.

Like the campaigns against street cruising and hip hop graffiti, the campaigns to eradicate the public presence of street gangs mix such moments of violent, disrespectable racism with the seemingly respectable politics of urban development and public safety. As Phoenix officials move to reproduce California's gang injunction model in their own minority neighborhoods, for example, the father of one boy identified as a "known" gang member links the injunction targeting his son to the redevelopment of downtown Phoenix and the building of the new Bank One Ballpark. "Since the stadium went up, they have been harassing the neighborhood more," he says. "They are trying to make us a parking lot" (in Harker 1999, B5).

Toward Spatial Justice, Social Justice, and the Dismantling of Petit Apartheid

The public controversies surrounding street cruisers, hip hop graffiti writers, and urban street gangs all reveal complex threads of ethnic inequality and injustice entangled in the cultural spaces of the city. In these spaces, new aggressions and indignities against ethnic minorities are invented, new patterns of petit apartheid enforced, new forms of "ethnic cleansing" promoted such that minority populations are removed, by the force of law and money, from particular spaces and situations. Significantly, this ethnic cleansing is at the same time a cultural cleansing; as economic, political, and legal authorities work to remake and recapture the public spaces of the city, they work also to control public perception, to remove from new spaces of consumption and development images of alternative ethnic identity. Moments of petit apartheid and everyday discrimination, of microaggression and macroaggression, intersect in the cultural spaces of the city—and do so in such a way that each moment constitutes (Henry and Milovanovic 1996) and contributes to the other. Together, these moments of spatial and ethnic injustice coalesce into expanded webs of social control, and into expanded arrangements of petit apartheid aimed at ethnic minorities and the public identities they inscribe in the spaces of the city.

In this sense, emerging forms of contemporary economic development and urban redevelopment, the increasing gentrification of urban areas and segregation of urban populations, suggest not only a growing class division between rich and poor, but the ever-expanding practice of day-to-day petit apartheid by public officials and criminal justice agents. Yet, in the same way that Georges-Abeyie's concept of petit apartheid alerts us to the fact that racial inequality and discrimination are reproduced and re-enforced through day-to-day spatial, cultural, and economic practices, it alerts us also to the opposite: that petit apartheid can begin to be confronted and dismantled through everyday spatial, cultural, and economic practices as well. Put more simply, if injustice operates at the level of everyday interaction, and within everyday spatial arrangements, then justice can be sought, and fought for, within these same quotidian domains. In fact, the very experiences of those caught up in contemporary cultural space battles—hip hop graffiti writers, gang members, and others—suggest that resistance to petit apartheid can indeed emerge in the streets and spaces, in the everyday cultural and economic politics, of the city.

Urban kids in the U.S. and other countries, for example, are building a Youth Peace Movement out of a combination of "union (politics), street culture, and indigenous activism, along with racial/ethnic participation." Their goal is to build a grass-roots movement that taps the "transformational capabilities inherent in youth" as a way of "bringing peace to the streets in constructive ways" (Childs 1997, 249, 251, 255). Other activists have orchestrated a growing street gang truce in the U.S., and along with this are not only developing resources to combat everyday police violence, but supporting projects "to hire jobless youth to recycle waste plastic into sturdy dome-homes for the homeless," and to construct "neighborhood 'cooperative zones' as an alternative to the cruel hoax of 'enterprise zones'" (Zinzun 1997, 265). Artists like Judy Baca continue to bring together hip hop graffiti writers and other young people from diverse ethnic backgrounds to create public murals celebrating ethnic heritage and cultural history; and other like-minded activists organize campaigns to confront and even illicitly alter alcohol and tobacco billboards targeting young Blacks and the urban spaces in which they live (Lippard 1990; see Sanchez-Tranquilino 1995).

Heeding Georges-Abeyie's call for "a criminological and criminal justice theory which is grounded in the experiential reality of non-whites" (1990b, 32), though, it is not enough simply to describe such anti-apartheid activities; it is important also to begin to build a grounded theory (Glaser and Strauss, 1967) of petit apartheid, and alternatives to it, out of the very words and experiences of those most directly involved. And so, by way of conclusion, we can consider some analytic insights offered not by academic criminologists, but by street kids, ethnic activists, and others confronting petit apartheid in the spaces of their daily lives. Mbanna Kantako, victim of a police beating that left him blinded, has gone on to organize Black Liberation Radio in Springfield, Illinois, and in so doing to pioneer the larger progressive microradio movement. Designed initially to promote tenants' rights and economic well-being, and to monitor and report on everyday police misconduct, the radio station soon developed into a force for community education and organization, and gave rise to similar stations in other communities. In their poem "'Ghetto Radio' Rap Song," Kantako's own children analyze this evolution of alternative sonic space:

It came from the projects	They say the revolution won't be televised
Where they put us all to die	They said this not long ago
Where they treated us like	But if you're ever in the place called
dogs	Springfield
We call it genocide....	You can see it on the radio.

(Kantako, Kantako, and Kantako, 1998, 104-105)

Michael Zinzun, himself a victim of police violence, chairperson of the Coalition Against Police Abuse, and architect of the emerging street gang truce, likewise argues for the transformative power of everyday street politics, and for a larger movement based on "linking the local, national, and international struggles for social justice and environmental justice" (Zinzun 1997, 261).

In the same way, hip hop graffiti writers themselves understand that their graffiti not only inscribes ethnic identity in the cultural spaces of the city, but itself becomes a form of activism, offering a powerful medium for confronting everyday violence, resisting petit apartheid, and transcending the social, cultural, and economic partitions that petit apartheid erects (Ferrell 1995). Echoing my own experiences with graffiti writers around the country, Crayone argues that "People don't know this, but graffiti gets people out of gangs. The media has it like we're all gangsters.... Graffiti kept me out of trouble with gangs. That makes no sense to a person who has never lived in the ghetto, but, what do you want, the kid to have a gun or a spray can in his hand?" Even more to the point, Sound One notes that "For me graffiti represents a way to instantly transcend governmental oppression (and its ignorance), social and racial barriers, and material possessions. It is also a way to take part in a movement which connects people from all over the world, regardless of personal differences, in a way nothing else can" (Walsh 1996, 17, 30).

As it turns out, the lessons offered by Georges-Abeyie and his concept of petit apartheid, and by the related notion of cultural space, are understood as well by graffiti writers and gang members, by ethnic activists and organizers, by Mbanna Kantako and Michael Zinzun, by Crayone, and Sound One:

Ethnicity and identity are forged in the spaces of daily life.

The everyday insults of petit apartheid must be met by everyday resistance.

Social justice demands spatial justice.

7

African American Interest in Law Enforcement: A Consequence of Petit Apartheid?

Lee E. Ross

Introduction

Today, as in previous decades, scholars from various disciplines engage in constructive dialogue of whether the criminal justice system is racist and discriminatory in its treatment of African Americans and other people of color. Wilbanks (1990), for instance, claimed that "studies available at various points in the criminal justice system fails to support the view that racial discrimination [was] pervasive" (1990, 9). In this sense, he concluded that the belief in a racist criminal justice system was a *myth*. His contentions prompted a litany of critical responses from his detractors — mostly criminologists — who questioned not only his methodology and conclusions, but his abilities to remain objective (see Daly 1994; Georges-Abeyie 1990; Mann 1998 1990; Miller 1996; Zatz 1990). Among his many critics was Georges-Abeyie (1990) who held that Wilbanks', foci on criminal justice [processes], per se, obscures and misdirects attention from significant contemporary forms of racism within the criminal justice system; that which he refers to as "petit apartheid." In the view of Georges-Abeyie, Wilbanks was barking up the wrong tree if he (or any other seriously-minded scholar) wished to test hypotheses of racism in the criminal justice system. Moreover, Wilbanks' general refusal to focus on informal processes — regarded as discriminatory, discretionary, and punitive acts — explains his failure to support counter-claims of racism. Georges-Abeyie describes the informal processes as:

> ....the everyday insults, rough and brutal treatment, and unnecessary stops, questions, and searches of Blacks; the lack of civility

faced by Black suspects/arrestees; the quality, clarity, and objectivity of the judges' instructions to the jury when a Black arrestee is on trial; the acceptance of lesser standards of evidence in cases that result in the conviction of Black arrestees, as well as numerous other punitively discretionary acts by law enforcement and correctional officers as well as jurists (p. 12).

For those familiar with the term "apartheid," it probably conjures up images of a South African policy based on racial segregation and the supremacy of whites. There, the purpose of apartheid was separation of the races; not only of whites from nonwhites, but also of nonwhites from each other, and, among the Africans (called Bantu in South Africa), of one group from another. Georges-Abeyie's coining and usage of the term "petit apartheid" conveys similar meaning of separating and distinguishing among the types of justice accorded people of color, however subtle and informal.

One thesis of this essay is that the current discourse of criminology and criminal justice conceivably alters the thinking and perspectives of Black students and later their career goals. This essay proceeds from the assumption that people of color—more so than others—appreciate and acknowledge the appearance and manifestations of petit apartheid, its degrees of complexity, its subtlety and manner of operation. Beyond mere recognition, however, this essay attempts to explore the possibility of negative consequences and societal repercussions that could result from a confluence of negative images, personal experiences, and prior research concerning differential and discriminatory treatment of people of color in the criminal justice system. In doing so, it maintains that "petit apartheid" may have an invidious effect on the career aspirations of many African Americans who, otherwise, may have chosen a career in law enforcement.

Consequences of Petit Apartheid?

While Georges-Abeyie used "petit apartheid" to refer to informal processes that are not easily measured, other researchers have followed suit in their use of interchangeable terms, such as "interaction effects" (Zatz 1990) and "macroaggressions" (Russell 1996). Beyond our preferred nomenclature, one has to wonder: what effect, if any, does educating students about the realities of crime and justice affect their career aspirations of working "for" the criminal justice system, especially within law enforcement. As a student of color attending a lecture in an introductory criminal justice course, how are they affected to learn that, for instance, when cops fire their weapons, they are more likely to fire at a minority and when deadly force is used, it is most often used against a minority, and that minorities are over-represented in arrest statistics (see Walker, Spohn, and DeLone 1996). Moreover, minorities are less likely to post bail; more likely to be prosecuted, and more likely to be sentenced to a period of incarceration—rather than receiving shorter probationary sentences (Reiman 1998). And in capital cases, Blacks are more likely to receive the death sentence when the victim is white (Baldus and Woodworth 1998). Even in terms of drug policy, for example, the plight of African Americans is no less different. According to the National Institute on Drug Abuse, "although only 12% of those using illegal drugs are Black, 44% of those arrested for simple possession and 57% of those arrested for sales are Black" (cf. Monk 1998, 180).

Pretend, if you will, you are a young—more than likely impressionable—African American male sitting there absorbing this information to go along with a panoply of knowledge and likewise personal experiences along these lines. Imagine further, that during the course of a semester, you are referred to as "an endangered species, an at-risk male" and the product of "a lost generation" (admitted to college through affirmative action and succeeding on the bases of "social promotions"). Adding insult to injury you come to the sudden realization—an epiphany of sort—that of all the race/sex categories, the chances of an African American male being victimized by homicide are six times greater than whites. While Blacks may have feared the Ku Klux Klan in the past, in the case of homicide they are wiser to fear each other as you learn further that 94% of Black victims are killed by Blacks (BJS 2000). Equally disheartening is that African Americans are seven times more likely than whites to *commit* homicide. Furthermore, since you are in college, you must have discovered by now that as of 1995, more young African American men nationwide were in prison than in college (Wolpert 1999).

Of course, beyond the negative portrayals of racism and discrimination against Blacks in the justice systems, the entire social legacy of Black experiences in America and its effects are important as they weigh heavily on your mind. In a recent visit to Indiana University, you understand that Dr. William Oliver, an African American professor of crime and justice, took time to elaborate some of these consequences with you. He is quoted as saying:

> One of the great tragedies associated with prejudice and racial discrimination against Black people is the negative effect it has had on how Black people view their worth as human beings. Through the manipulation of the educational system, religion, folklore, vaudeville shows, radio and television programs, film and various print media, the Black image in the minds of Black people has been

severely distorted by the construction and dissemination of un-
truths and stereotypes (1996, 81).

After considering the knowledge, information, and experiences acquired
from inside and outside the classroom, imagine what your response might
be when asked by your professor to seriously consider a career in law enforcement. A consideration of the professor's idea, however, may not be as
predictable and unequivocal as one might expect as African Americans—
like white Americans—are not a homogenous group but a collection of individuals. Moreover, the answer, in part, may depend on whether the individual identifies with minority populations, perceives minorities as victims
of racial and social injustice, and is of the opinion that through ones in-
volvement and participation, they can make a difference. Furthermore, the
salience of social background—even level of social consciousness—cannot
be overstated. When matters of financial necessity (i.e., employment needs)
are thrown into the mixture, career decisions are further complicated.

Nonetheless, working in law enforcement carries certain social consequences as some individuals subscribe to the notion they are some how
"sell outs' aligning with the enemy in a system regarded by many as in-
herently racist, dangerously evil, and morally bankrupt. For instance, the
role of Christopher Darden in the trial of O.J. Simpson was seen as somewhat of an analogue for all Black prosecutors; Darden was seen as an
Uncle Tom, a collaborator with the white man and his bigoted system
(Wolpert 1999). In this context, one need not be regarded as militant to appreciate the admonitions of the late Malcolm X whose thoughts on joining
the system (i.e., the U.S. military) are summarized accordingly: Why go to
war to defend and preserve a country that will only further oppress and en-
slave my people? In a similar vein, Paul Butler, a law professor at George
Washington University, espouses the practice of jury nullification as tool
for empowering Blacks and bringing some sort of fairness to the criminal
justice system (Butler 1995). In outright defiance, he adds:

> If African Americans simply followed the law because Whites told
> them to, they'd still be slaves…The law doesn't Come from God.
> It comes from people like Jesse Helms and Newt Gingrich (c.f.
> Biskupic 1999).

While sentiments reflecting one's refusal to work for a system perceived
as racist continue to be an unfortunate reality, it serves to illustrate the far-
reaching consequences of "petit apartheid." For Elijah Anderson (1994),
the effects of petit apartheid are far reaching—even providing a partial explanation for the increased use of guns and lethal violence among African
Americans. Fearing that they would become victims of police use of deadly
force, some Blacks readily arm themselves and adopt a attitude of either

"kill or be killed." Moreover, "even decent people in inner-city neighbor-hoods are so distrustful of the police that they feel they have no choice but to take matters of personal defense into their own hands" (c.f. White 1999). Other consequences are further explored in the following section.

Professional Aspirations

....the policeman moves through Harlem, therefore, like an occu-pying soldier in a bitterly hostile country; which is precisely what, and where he is, and the reason he walks in twos and threes (James Baldwin, *Nobody Knows My Name*).

In the last millenium, one of the most important events took place on October 16, 1995 in Washington, DC. Today, we know it as the Million Man March (followed five years later by the Million Family March). For many Black men, this historic event provided opportunities to commune, to atone, and to envision a future filled with hope, peace, and prosperity; one that would forever alter the conditions of violence, poverty, and despair. Just as time spent incarcerated provides ample opportunity to enhance one's criminal proclivities, the Million Man March provided equal oppor-tunities to exchange personal and anecdotal experiences with the criminal justice system, conveying the impression it had accomplished its mission in a decent and respectable manner.

Yet, despite its many positive attributes, one cannot help but to wonder how many (of the "purported" million Black men present) aspired to a ca-reer in law enforcement? More specifically, how many were employed in law enforcement at that time? Before venturing an educated guess, one should realize that at the time of the march, more than one in four African American young men of age 20-29 was under criminal supervision na-tionwide (e.g., Monk 1998). Recent studies indicate an estimated 45 mil-lion United States residents—one in five—will have face-to-face contact with law enforcement officers in a given year (BJS 1997). As minorities are known to be over-represented in arrest statistics, one can reasonably spec-ulate that more than half of the men in attendance—innumerable juveniles as well—had previous experience with the justice system.

Maybe to the surprise of only a few recently arrived immigrants, African Americans in general, harbor less than favorable attitudes toward the crim-inal justice system. According to a recent USA Today/CNN/Gallop poll, 66% of African Americans believed the criminal justice system is racist and only 32% believe it is not racist (e.g., Monk 1998, 190). That being the case, one can reiterate the previous question: How many Black men at-tending the march aspired to a career in law enforcement? While considering the question, it might prove useful to explore and critique the mindset of *any* Black man who would purposefully reject an opportunity to become part of a system that could conceivably prove professionally satisfying and financially rewarding. Surely, to turn down job opportunities of this nature is tantamount to "cutting off one's nose to spite one's face." Still, others may regard working for a system perceived as racist as undesirable. Moreover, they might question whether they can genuinely invest their heart and souls in a profession, such as policing, where they may become complicit in furthering the plight and oppression of other Black people.

With each passing day, are African Americans so affected by "petit apartheid" that their interests in working for the system gradually diminishes? Unquestionably, this is one possibility—but there are other possibilities as well. For many African Americans with no history of drug use or prior felony convictions law enforcement opportunities are difficult to ignore, despite ones views on how unjust a system might be. Toward this end, these individuals realize that employment opportunities in criminal justice are widely scattered among federal, state, municipal, and local agencies. Special agent positions, as an example, are usually attractive—regardless of the agency. Generally, once hired and having completed a period of probation, greater career opportunities become available. For instance, careers within the Federal Bureau of Investigation include fingerprint specialist, crime laboratory technician, explosives examiner, document expert, polygraph operator, ballistics technician, and computer operator among many others. With rare exceptions, media depictions and Hollywood portrayals often glamorize the FBI, making it all the more desirable, regardless of one's racial identity, perceptions, and experiences with petit apartheid. In fact, since the FBI is a federal agency, the likelihood of the average citizen having a negative encounter—or any encounter for that matter—is minimal. Therefore, African Americans and other persons of color are, indeed, interested in these career opportunities. Objectively, their interests in the FBI might surprise those of us all too familiar with the infamous—clearly racist—reputation of its former director, J. Edgar Hoover, who kept African American leaders under close surveillance (e.g., Malcolm X and Dr. Martin Luther King, Jr.) and is suspected of being implicated in their assassinations.

As of June 1998, the latest available data, Federal agencies employed about 83,000 full time personnel with roughly 51,000 assigned to either "police response and patrol" or criminal investigative and enforcement functions" (BJS 2000). Although the FBI is the third largest employee of federal officers (i.e., 11,285), it continues to languish as an agency refusing to embrace persons of color. African Americans have found it difficult to gain entry and even more difficult to advance once hired.

Closer to home, minority interest in local law enforcement has actually increased despite documented instances of police corruption, illegal shake-downs, false arrests, excessive force, and disproportionate use of deadly force against mostly minority alleged offenders. The latest available data indicate that as of June 1997, local police departments had an estimated 531,496 full-time employees, including 420,000 sworn personnel. Racial and ethnic minorities comprised 21.5% of full-time sworn officers in local police departments in 1997. This compared to 19.1% in 1993, 17% in 1990, and 14.6% in 1987 (BJS 2000). Although it is difficult to ascertain the exact percentage of Blacks within the category of "racial and ethnic minorities" it does appear that this type of law enforcement is attractive to some African Americans. Toward that end, how might a typical 24 year-old African American respond to a recent job announcement on the web-site of the New York Police Department?

> There has never been a better time to join the NYPD. The depart-ment is modernizing management, improving technology, and up-dating training. The NYPD leads the nation with the most dra-matic crime reduction in our time. The NYPD is making history by making New York the safest city in America and you can be a part it.

Black or Blue: Which are You?

Perhaps no words can articulate the current dilemma of African Amer-icans who aspire to law enforcement careers better than the provocative and challenging expression "if you are not part of the solution—you are part of the problem." In light of the aforementioned, some African Amer-icans regard instances of systemic discrimination, and racist police prac-tices (i.e., racial profiling) as an opportunity to become part of the solution. History reminds us that one way to correct a perceived injustice is to be-come active and work with the problem from within the system. The fa-miliarity of the approach embodies the age-old mantra "if you can't beat them—join them." For instance, if "driving while Black" (or DWB) is a reality for many Black motorists—and I have good reasons to believe it is—Black officers can provide protection against such practices when they become one of the men and women in blue. Few Black motorists would deny that if they are stopped (illegally), they would much rather prefer being stopped by someone who looks like them, as this tends to minimize suspicions of racial profiling—though not necessarily. The fear, however, for purposes of our discussion, is that perceptions and experiences with petit apartheid can also serve as an instant "turn-off" to many potential African American recruits. Consequently, it results in the continued under-representation of minorities in the system, which, in my estimate, ironically forms the bases for petit apartheid.

Conceivably, the intermingling of American ideals of justice with one's desire to correct injustice provides the impetus and catalyst for African American interests in law enforcement careers. Here, notions of personal integrity assume center stage, flanked by the vanguards of peace-making criminology; after all, we need not arrest everyone who transgresses the law. For African Americans with lifelong aspirations for law enforcement, they would probably embrace the mythical ideals of our Founding Fathers (who had much to say about crime and justice in the Bill of Rights). It should be easy to imagine a scenario where African American police officers object to practices of racial profiling because they recognize—as do others—that it is a constitutional violation. Imagine further the challenge of educating fellow officers—most of whom are white—who may object to this concept of professionalism and Black officers' blatant refusal *to toe the thin blue line.*

It is equally conceivable, however, that others—given ideological, philosophical, and class-based differences (with "John Q. Public" on the streets)—may even espouse racial profiling because their common sense and prior experiences tells them, for example, *that if it walks like a felon and talks like a felon—it probably is a felon.* Therefore, assumptions of improved treatment of Black suspects at the hands of Black officers are specious at best. As law enforcement professionals, officers of all persuasions are expected to uphold the law, and given the ever watchful eye of supervisory personnel—many of whom are Caucasian—Black officers can be especially "tough" with Black citizens to avoid an appearance of favoritism. Along these lines, Black officers, like persons in general, seek acceptance and approval among their peers. Few can deny the pressures to conform to established, albeit unprofessional, procedures of administering *street justice.* Consequently, when Black citizens confront Black officers with familiar refrains of *"Yo, can't you give a brother a break?"* the answer—more times than not—is unequivocally "no!" Through time, some people of Color may perceive Black officers as no better—if not worse—than white officers in the under-enforcement and over-enforcement of crime in Black communities. As a result, some Black officers may find themselves in a no win situation where divided loyalties threaten their sense of belonging, question their moral convictions, and undermine their ethical obligations to both their profession and to their community.

Conclusion

The fate of many African Americans haphazardly rests in the hands of police officers whose discretion to stop them—oftentimes without probable cause—appears somewhat preordained based on inescapable biological features immersed in a world of structural inequality. While some Blacks remain fearful of an uncertain future, the past provides a virtual litany of unpleasant encounters with police that forces us all to realize that we could have been the victims of ostensibly racist law enforcement practices. Which African American male does not run the risk of being the next Rodney King who, you'll remember, was beaten bloody? And given the wrong set of circumstances, who, among us, will be any more fortunate than Abner Louima, sodomized with a broken broomstick while in police custody? Will I—or you for that matter—escape the fate of Amadou Diallo, who was killed in a haze of gunfire by NYPD's *elite* street crimes unit? Perhaps, the reality of petit apartheid is so heavily ensconced in racist attitudes and behaviors that it simply refuses to go away. And yet, racism, for both Georges-Abeyie (1990) and Quindlen (2000), is a topic few Americans wish to acknowledge. Quindlen's (2000) contemporary examples speak volumes as she recalls:

> [P]olice officers looking for drug dealers in New York threw four professional men in jail—including, ironically, the Black actor who played Coalhouse Walker, harassed by bigots in the musical *Ragtime* (p. 77).

Realizing that this could happen to anyone of us (especially African Americans), it leaves one to wonder along biblical lines: where would any of us be if not for the Grace of God?

In conclusion, the plight of African Americans, as presented here, can be summarized as nothing less than a catch-22 situation. The catch is simple. African Americans have good reason to be leery of police. They are reasonable to expect consternation from fellow African Americans in their aspirations to join the men and women in blue. After all, police are blue first and Black second. Yet, on the other hand, people of color who fear continued discriminatory police practices would gain much if more African Americans would join law enforcement. If nothing else, it may provide peace of mind in knowing that the next time they are stopped, the officer will at least look like them with (an assumed) greater appreciation for what they experience on a daily basis in the form of petit apartheid.

8

Racial Derogation in Prosecutors' Closing Arguments[1]

Sheri Lynn Johnson

Bennett, who is African American, was sentenced [to death] by an all white jury... The prosecutors told jurors that [the victim's encounter with Bennett] was "like running into King Kong on a bad day." (Closing argument by South Carolina prosecutor in 2000) (Columbia State 2000).

And scripture tells us there is a time to rend or reap what one has sown and he needs to know that, quote, this is not another case of niggeritous. (Prosecutor's closing argument reviewed by Alabama Court of Criminal Appeals in 1996).[2]

Yeah, you can bet the parents wanted a conviction. This is every mother's nightmare. Leave your daughter for an hour and a half, and you walk back in, and here's some black, military guy on top of your daughter. (Prosecutor's closing argument reviewed by Hawaii Supreme Court in 1999).[3]

There are no "race shield laws." Nor are there other measures that adequately curb the use of racial imagery by prosecutors in their closing arguments. Moreover, in contrast to the political and scholarly climate that preceded the adoption of *rape* shield laws, there is no storm of protest on this front. (Earle 1992, DeBrota 1989). Perhaps the lack of attention to the use of racial imagery in criminal cases stems from a perception that resort to such imagery is rare, but it is not. Or perhaps disinterest may be traced

---

1. This chapter is an updated excerpt from Sheri Lynn Johnson, Racial Imagery in Criminal Cases, 67 TULANE L. REV. 1739 (1993). The article addresses use of racial imagery by other defense counsel, judges, and jurors as well as by prosecutors.

2. Ivery v. State, 686 So. 2d 495(Ala. 1996).

3. State v. Rogan, 984 P. 2d 1231 (Haw. 1999).

to the belief that the likely effects of such imagery will seldom sway the jury as intended, and may even backfire, benefitting the object of the imagery, though available evidence is to the contrary. A third non-invidious interpretation might be proffered: People are unaware that the law is largely silent here, and they assume that whatever the frequency of racial argument by prosecutors and whatever its effect might be on juries, injustices are corrected by the courts, but this assumption too would be erroneous.

There is also selective indifference to consider (Brest 1976, 7-8). Half of the population is female, and many women could identify with the rape victim cross-examined on the details of her sexual life to facilitate summation arguments that she was a consenting whore, but there are fewer people of color to identify with racial derogation by prosecutors. Another obvious explanation is self-interested denial. Daniel Georges-Abeyie's construct of "petit apartheid" both illuminates these racial arguments and helps to explain why they remain unredressed: "the everyday insults... of blacks" are obscured by formal fairness (Georges-Abeyie 1987, 11-12). Acknowledging the continuing legacy of racism is painful and unpleasant, at least for white people, and for many persons of color as well (Bell 1992, 13); it implies that many of us do not deserve all we have, that our good fortune is gained through the exploitation of, and microaggressions upon, others (Davis 1989). It is particularly hard when we are confronted with the racism of—and the manipulation of racism by—a "professional" such as a prosecutor. Maybe we not only benefit from skin privilege, but also tolerate the privileging in our own ranks. Looking closely at racial imagery used by professionals can compound this discomfort, for when we examine the speech patterns and images other professionals use, comparisons to our own everyday remarks will nag at the edges of our thought. Maybe we do more than tolerate skin privileging, maybe we practice it (Lawrence 1987, 339-44).

More vile explanations are possible, but I nevertheless choose to proceed upon a cautiously optimistic assumption: At least *part* of the inattention to racial imagery stems from (more or less) non-invidious ignorance. This chapter, therefore, attempts to redress some of that ignorance and, for the bulk of it, I proceed by assuming that information and logical argument may be persuasive. In the conclusion, however, I return to the possibility of more invidious reasons for the void, considering whether the self-righteousness and self-interest of white people preclude the redressing of ignorance in this area.

If this introduction sounds angry, I do not apologize. I do, however, wish to make clear that the object of my anger is not other, but same: my culture, my language, indeed, my self. I am white. As I began writing the immediately preceding paragraph, what came to my mind first was "Other, darker, explanations are possible." That was, of course, both the right and the wrong image. It is impossible for me to begin without at least this much candor: I have met the enemy, and she is us.

Setting the Stage for Racial Derogation by Prosecutors

Racial imagery can be conveyed in pictures, stories, examples and generalizations. These visual and auditory experiences may themselves generate a racial image, or they may recall for the observer racial imagery to which she was exposed at an earlier time. Because race is such a salient characteristic in our society (Brewer 1988; Smith and Zarate 1990), a juror will notice the race of the defendant, the witnesses, the attorneys, the judge, and other jurors. What each juror will "see" when she observes an African American judge, a white defendant, a Latino witness, or an Asian American prosecutor will be affected by what happens in the courtroom, but what she "sees" happening in the courtroom will be affected by her prior exposure to racial imagery. The racial imagery that affects a particular jury's decision making process is therefore impossible to catalog.

We can, however, acknowledge a vast and varied set of racial experiences and racial images with which jurors begin. Indeed, were there not such preexisting images, there would be little incentive for either party to invoke racial images during the course of the trial. Therefore, we do not consider how bias is *created* by prosecutors, but note various ways in which preexisting racial images are repeated, recalled, and reshaped.

Closing arguments permit both defense counsel and the prosecuting attorney to summarize and argue from the evidence. While neither side may argue facts outside the evidence and both must refrain from arguments that "inflame" the jury, passion, flamboyance, and rhetorical flourish are permitted. Within the bounds of a proper summation, a prosecutor may repeat and stress racial imagery used by witnesses or he may introduce new imagery by his words, metaphors, or demeanor. Moreover, prosecuting attorneys often stray beyond the bounds of a proper summation without a mistrial being declared. Sometimes defense counsel hesitates to emphasize the offensive remark by her objection; even when she does object, the judge is likely to merely admonish the jury to disregard the offensive remarks.

Specific Stereotypes and Fears

There are a variety of racial stereotypes for each disfavored ethnic group. I do not attempt to review all of the possible stereotypes that might be invoked, for hypotheticals might be constructed for almost any stereotyped characteristic. Rather, I start by categorizing real and relatively recent cases, acquired through a systematic search of reported cases, none of which precede the post-civil rights era, and then extrapolate a bit from them about cases that are probably occurring but about which we do not have reliable information.

Racial Images of Evil

Most starkly, black may be identified with evil and white with good. Perhaps because the imagery is so extreme, invocations of it tend to be somewhat indirect. It was a "black Sunday" when the black defendant set out after his white victims.[4] The prosecutor in another case involving an African American defendant, described the victim as a "nice white lady."[5]

Racial images of violence

Closely related is the image of African Americans as more violent, more criminal than whites. Thus one prosecutor said the defendant "had to play Superfly," alluding to a fictional black criminal.[6] Another prosecutor, seeking to impeach the veracity of the defendant's contention that he believed the three arresting plain clothes officers were muggers, repeatedly argued that the African American defendant could not have believed that white men were muggers.[7] In one case with a black defendant and black victim, the prosecutor discussed at some length the prevalence of black crime generally and of black-on-black crime in particular, arguing that this Detroit pattern should not be permitted to reach Joliet;[8] in another such case, the prosecutor said "Ninety percent of all murders are committed by blacks on blacks" and "It's time to say 'We're not going to allow this kind of conduct to go on in our city anymore.'"[9] In yet another case, the prosecutor argued that the local drug market was being taken over by Jamaicans and introduced expert testimony to that effect; the only relevance of this as-

4. Louisiana v. Wilson, 404 So. 2d 968, 969 (1981).

5. Louisiana v. Greene, 542 So. 2d 156, 157 (La. App. 1989).

6. Smith v. Indiana, 516 N.E. 2d 1055, 1064 (1987).

7. State v. Thomas, 514 N.Y.S.2d 91 (App. Div. 1987). See also, People v. Traylor, 487 NE2d 1040 (Ill. 1985) (prosecutor argued that police officers' approach to stolen vehicle could be explained by fact that they were "white policemen in a black neighborhood").

8. Illinois v. Lurry, 395 N.E. 2d 1234 (Ill. 1979).

9. State v. Noel, 693 S.W. 2d 317 (Mo. 1985). See also State v. Franklin, 526 SW 2d 86 (Mo.App. 1975) (in a robbery case with a black defendant, prosecutor remarked in closing that victims of 85 percent of crime in the city are the people who have to live in black areas or who do live there).

sertion to the case was the Jamaican ancestry of the defendants.[10] In a peculiar twist on the propensity argument, a prosecutor argued that the defendant must have entered the robbed premises because the co-defendant would never have let "him sit out there—I don't mean to be racial about this...[but do you think he would leave]...a black guy out there in a car, or a big car while a robbery is going on?"[11]

Racial images related to violence are not limited to African Americans. In a case involving recent Italian immigrants, *both* defense counsel and prosecutor argued about Al Capone and "The Godfather";[12] in another case involving American Indian defendants, the prosecutor argued that "when you see an Indian that drinks liquor, you see a man that can't handle it" and that such drinking leads to violence;[13] in another case the prosecutor asked the defendant, "Isn't it true that in gypsy practice it is OK to lie and cheat and steal if you can get away with it?"[14]

People of Color as Subhuman

Equally abhorrent are portrayals of persons of color as animal, or subhuman in some other way. Animal imagery is actually quite common in prosecutor's summations, perhaps because not all courts deem it impermissible. In a few recent cases, the racial import of these terms is clear;[15] in

---

10. United States v. Doe, 903 F 2d 16 (D.C. Cir. 1990). See also, Russell v. State, 69 Md. App. 554, 518 A. 2d 11081,1085 (Md. 1987) (prosecutor refers to "Jamaican drug trafficking" in his opening statement, and police officer in his testimony about his specialty as a narcotics officer).

11. State v. Snowden, 675 P2d 289 (Ariz. 1983).

12. Commonwealth v. Graziano 368 Mass 325, 331 N.E.2d 808 (1975). See also State v. Filipov, 118 Ariz. 319, 576 P.2d 507 (1978)(prosecutor refers to recent immigrant as "gypsy" and compares him to Sicilians); Haas v. State, 247 SE 2d 507 (Ga.), cert. Den. 440 U.S. 922 (1978) (prosecutor repeatedly refers to an alias used in the indictment, to an Italian connection, and to the defendant as a "Sicilian.)

13. Soap v. Carter, 632 F.2d 872,878 (10th Cir. 1980) (Seymour, J., dissenting). See also, United States v. Rodriguez Cortez, 949 F 2d 532 (1st Cir. 1991) (trial court admitted evidence of defendant's Colombian identity as probative of his membership in a narcotics conspiracy with other Colombian members).

14. Stanton v. State, 349 So. 2d 761 (Fla. 1977).

15. See eg. State v. Wilson, 404 So.2d 968 1981) district attorney's remarks contained repeated references to "whitey" and "white honkies" in connection with defendant's supposed characterization of whites and to "animals" as a description of the defendants); People v. Nightengale, 168 Ill. App. 3d 968, 972, 523 N.E.2d 136, 119 Ill. Dec. 668 (1988) (description in text); State v. Wilson, 404 So.2d 357 (La. App 5th Cir. 1981) (references to black defendants as animals in case filled with direct and indirect appeals to racial prejudice of all-white jury).

one the prosecutor characterized the defendant as "a debased animal" and "scum" who committed crimes in "our streets" and not in "some ghetto."[16] In most cases complaining of animal imagery, the court does not discuss the ethnicity of the defendant; occasionally, however, the defendant's name or other details of a particular case make it clear that courts are ignoring the interaction of such imagery with the defendant's race.[17] Sometimes the reference to sub-humanity is more oblique, as when a prosecutor asked whether it was reasonable to believe the victim would consent to sex with "....*that?*"[18] Other degrading, dehumanizing imagery includes the use of the word "n*****,"[19] or other ethnic slurs[20] and the practice of referring to a minority race defendant by his or her first name.[21]

16. People v. Nightengale, 972, 523 N.E.2d 136, (Ill. 1988).

17. See e.g., People v. Rivera, 426 N.Y.S. 2d 785,786 (App. Div. 1980)(referring to defendants as "wolves of this soicety"). For an older such case, see Miller v. State, 163 S.E.2d 730, 734 (Ga. 1968); see also State v. Wilson, 404 So.2d 968 (La. 1981) (court finds no racial prejudice in black defendant case with three summation references to animals); Commonwealth v. Layton, 376 NE 2d 150 (Mass. 1978) (farfetched to think argument about streets of commonwealth becoming a "jungle" were racially motivated in black defendant robbery case).

18. Thomas v. State, 419 So 2d 634 (Fla. 1982). See also Patterson v. Commonwealth, 555 SW2d 607 (Ky App 1977) (in black defendant-white victim case, in which prosecutor said "[I]t's hard for me to tell black people apart," he also said rape is not conduct befitting "a member of the human race").

19. I am neither willing to use that word, nor able to see a need for its use. Cases in which that epithet is used still occur, albeit less often than they used to. See New York v. Walker, 411N.Y.S.2d 377 (1978); Kornegay v. State, 329 S.E.2d 601 (Ga. 1985); Thornton v. Beto, 470 F2d 657 (5th Cir 1972), cert. den. 411 U.S. 920); Sparks v. State, 563 S.W.2d 564 (Tenn. Crim. App.1978). See also McBride v. State, 338 So.2d 567 (Fla. Dist. Ct. App. 1976) (prosecutor elicited testimony of use of ethnic slur by white defendant, presumably to offend two black jurors).

20. In State v. Martinez, 658 P2d 428(N.M. 1983), the prosecutor referred to the defendant as a "chola punk," a term which I might not repeat if I either knew what it meant or how to signal it. In People v. Wilson, 198 NW2d 424 (Mich. 1972), both the prosecutor and the defense counsel referred to the defendant and his companion as "colored" and in State v. Parker,, 509 P 2d 272 (N.M. 1973) the prosecutor referred to black persons as "colored".

21. In Hamilton v. Alabama, 376 U.S.650 (1963) (facts reported in Bell v. Maryland, 378 U.S. 226,248n.4(1964)) the Supreme Court reversed a contempt conviction against a black witness who refused to answer due to a solicitor's insistence on calling her by her first name. It would be a mistake to conclude that minority race defendants and witnesses are not presently so degraded; it just does not lead to published reports in most circumstances. The Rodney King beating case provided one example of a witness using a black adult's first name. The prosecutor corrected the witness. (I have not found a newspaper report of this fact, but it is recorded on courtroom tapes.) I suspect this is not unusual. One of my clients was referred to by the prosecutor in the course of an extremely inflammatory summation as "Pedro." People v. Pedro Arroyo, 431 N.E. 2d 271 (N.Y. 1982) See also State v. Torres, 554

Sexual Threat Imagery

In other cases, the supposed sexual appetite of, or the supposed sexual threat posed by black men, is played upon. In the rape case variation, the prosecutor argues, sometimes in hysterical terms,[22] that the victim, a white woman, would never have consented to have sex with the defendant because he is a black man.[23] In cases not involving sexual assault, sexual threat imagery is exploited when the prosecutor directs the jury's attention to a fact irrelevant to the case: that the black defendant has had one or more sexual relationships with white women.[24] The most extreme example of this is found in a 1987 Nevada case involving a death penalty hearing in which the prosecutor directed the jury's attention to the defendant's "preference for white women" and his "physical relationship" with a white woman.[25] Finally, in a case involving a white male victim, the prosecutor argued that the man had to be telling the truth because his story included an account of intercourse with a black woman and "if he is going to lie about anything else, he wouldn't admit having intercourse with a black woman."[26]

P2d 1069 (Wash. 1976) (repeatedly referring to defendants as Mexicans or Mexican Americans while referring to the complaining witness with the formal "Ms." or "Mrs.").

22. For repeated and extensive comments, see Reynolds v. Florida, 580 So 2d. 254 (Fla.1991). See also Miller v. North Carolina, 583 F.2d 701 (4th Cir. 1978) ("the average white woman abhors anything of [a sexual] nature that has to do with a black man").

23. State v. Thomas, 111 Utah Adv. Rep. 24, 777 P 2d 445 (1989); Miller v. North Carolina, 583 F.2d 701 (4th Cir. 1978)("the average white woman abhors anything of a sexual nature that had to do with a black man"); Reynolds v. Florida 580 So2d 254 1991); State v. Bautista, 30 Utah 2d 112, 514 P2d 530 (1973).See also State v. Mayhue, 653 SW 2d 227 (Mo. 1983) ("[N]o person in their right mind would want to remember three black men getting on her naked body...."); Rhoden v. State, 49 Ala App. 605, 274 So 2d 630 (1973)(in an interracial rape case replete with references by both prosecutor and defense counsel to white lady and "white woman," prosecutor told jury that if they believed complaining witness, they would have to believe that defendant "...took it, he got him a white woman").

24. Weddington v. State, 545 A. 2d 607 (1988); People v. Springs, 300 N.W. 2d 315 (Mich. 1980); Johnson v. Rose, 546 F. 2d 678 (6th Cir, 1976); U.S. v. Grey, 422 F.2d 1043 (6th Cir. 1970); People v. Nichols, 308 NE2d 848 (Ill. 1974); State v. Parker, 509 P2d 272 (N.M. 1973). See also State v. Deas, 212 SE 2d 693(N.C. App.), cert. Den., 287 NC 467, 215 SE2d 626(1975) (prosecutor argued that if motel operator had seen white woman in the car when black defendant was registering as man and wife, he would have remembered it because it don't happen in Transylvania County; it might happen in Charlotte, but it don't happen in Transylvania County").

25. Dawson v. State, 734 P 2d 221 (Nev. 1987). See also, People v. Nichols, 308 NE.2d 848 (Ill. 1974) (prosecutor's closing argument refers to fact that black defendant is married to a white woman).

26. People v. Richardson, 363 N.E.2d 924 (Ill. 1977).

Racial images of Dishonesty

Black dishonesty is another racial image that has been exploited by prosecutors. At one time it was relatively common to find arguments that African Americans are less trustworthy witnesses, and I found three cases in which the prosecutor made that argument quite directly. In one, the prosecutor said "Not one white witness has been produced in this case that contradicts [the white prosecution witness'] position in this case";[27] in the second, the prosecutor characterized the testimony of a black defense witness as "shucking and jiving on the stand;"[28] in the third, referring to the black defendant and his black witnesses as "street people," the prosecutor said "they lie every day."[29] One variation on the dishonesty image is that African Americans are likely to be lying when they testify for each other[30] and likely to be telling the truth when they testify against each other.[31] An interesting interracial twist on this argument is presented by a case where the prosecutor argued that the testimony of the defendant's alibi witness should be doubted because as a white woman living with a black man, she had faced a lot of social disapproval, and she would therefore be more likely to be willing to lie for him.[32]

Emphasizing Racial Divisions

The last specific brand of racial imagery found in the prosecutor misconduct cases I would call "us-them" imagery. In its most outrageous form, it pictures black on white violence as more horrible than other violence, implying that the jury must act to restrain future interracial crimes. Thus in one case with a black victim and a black defendant, the prosecutor said if the jury released the defendant, "maybe the next time it won't be a little black girl from the other side of the tracks...maybe it will be somebody that you know";[33] in one case, the prosecutor rhetorically asked the jury in a capital murder trial, "Can you imagine the fear that [the victim] went

---

27. Withers v. United States, 602 F.2d 124 (6th Cir. 1979).

28. Smith v. State, 516 N.E.2d 1055,1064 (Ind. 1987).

29. People v. Richardson, 363 N.E.2d 924 (Ill. 1977). See also State v. Kamel, 466 NE 2d 860 (Ohio 1984) (prosecutor argued that defense witnesses were unreliable by reason of their foreign birth in the Mideast).

30. People v. Richardson, 363 N.E.2d 924 (Ill. 1977); People v. Kong, 517 N.Y.S. 2d 71,72 (App. Div. 1987).

31. McFarland v. Smith, 611 F.2d 414,416 (2d Cir. 1979); People v. Bramlet, 569 N.E.2d 1139 (Ill. 1991).

32. State v. Terry, 582 SW2d 337 (Mo. 1979).

33. Kelly v. Stone 514 F.2d 18 (9th Cir. 1975).

through out with three blacks?"[34] In another case, the state's attorney characterized the defendant as scum who committed a crime "in our streets" and "not in some ghetto."[35] In a fourth case, the prosecutor argued that the defendant's homicidal act was caused by the racial tenets of the Black Muslim religion,[36] and in several cases, the prosecutor called on fears of racial revenge by arguing that black or Latino defendants with white victims were motivated by racial animosity despite the lack of any evidence regarding the defendant's motives.[37] There are also a number of cases in racial animosity is fueled by the attribution of an ethnic slur like "honkey" — often without basis in the record.[38]

The second form of us-them imagery focuses on how different "they" are; while this form might seem milder, some of these remarks are breathtakingly long and digressive descents into stereotypy. In one case, the transcription of the prosecutors racial remarks required two pages of the reporter, beginning with a discussion of whether the defendant would be considered a "n*****" in his own community."[39] In another case, the prosecutor discussed "colored" people as people who wear "exotic" hairstyles, straighten their hair, and wear unusual sideburns, as well arguing for the early sexual maturity black people and their inability to do or know things that are "commonplace for the ordinary person."[40] In a third case, previ-

---

34. Petition for a Writ of Certiorari, at 18, Russell v. Collins, 944 F2d 202 (5th Cir.) (No. AC692), cert. den., 112 S.Ct.30 (1991).

35. People v. Nightengale, 523 N.E.2d 136 (Ill. App.1988).

36. Commonwealth v. Mahdi, 448 N.E. 2d 704 (Mass.1983).

37. Carter v. Artis, 621 F. Supp. 40 (1985); State v. Snedecor, 294 So.2d 207 (La. 1974); State v. Jones, 283 So. 2d 476 (La. 1973); People v. Rivera,, 523 NYS2d 834 (App. Div. 1988); People v. Sales, 502 NE.2d 1221 (Ill. 1986). See also, People v. Flores, 398 NE 2d 1132 (Ill. 1979) (prosecutor argued that differences in nationality between defendants from Puerto Rico and victim from Mexico nay have motivated crime).

38. See eg. State v. Wilson, 404 So 2d. 968 (1981) ("whitey" and "white honkies"); U.S. v. Harvey, 756 F.2d 636 (1985) ("honkey");Dixon v. State 173 Ga. App. 280, 325 SW 2d 893 (1985) (prosecutor elicited inadmissible hearsay including defendant's purported reference to victim as "this honkey"); People v. Turner, 52 Ill. App. 3d 738, 367 NE2d 1365, 10 Ill. Dec. 599 (1977)(prosecutor falsely stated that black witness had said he was going to have a good time watching two black girls "beat up whitey"). Cf. McBride v. Florida, 338 So.2d 567 (Fla. 1976) ("n*****" accurately attributed to defendant in a case with black jurors). See also, United States v, Haynes, 466 F2d 1260 (5th Cir. 1972) (prosecutor said "burn, baby burn" to African American defendant).

39. People v. Walker, 411 N.Y.S. 2d 377 (App. Div. 1978).

40. Haynes v. McKendrick, 481 F. 2d 152 (2d Cir. 1973). See also Sparks v. State, 563 SW 2d 564 (Tenn. 1978) (digression on what the use of ethnic slurs mean between two black people, depending on whether or not white people are present); People v. Flores, 398 NE2d 1132 (Ill..1979) (referring to a defendant's Puerto Rican origins and a victim's Mexican ori-

ously mentioned for the prosecutor's argument that American Indians have a propensity for alcohol abuse and violence, the prosecutor also commented:

> You try to impress upon people that they can change—that they should change, and there is a decent way of going through life without violence, without committing crimes and still you can enjoy life and obtain things and goals in your life, but some people don't live this way and they won't live that way. That's what you have in this case. You have a class of [people] and a situation that exists that you and I can't change irrespective of what we do...but I submit to you that the facts surrounding this are typical of the community in which this accident occurred...and there is nothing you and I can do to change this situation, other than you can suggest with your verdict in this case what you want to do, what kind of standard you want to ask or set in this country.[41]

There is also an interracial twist to us-them imagery; for example, that a white defendant associates with black people and has had black witnesses testify for him has been the subject of demeaning prosecutorial comment.[42] This of course, is to be expected; petit apartheid, like its bigger, older brother, punishes the public crossing of racial lines by whites as well as by people of color.

Unnecessary References to Racial Identity

Finally, there are a large number of cases in which no specific racial imagery is called upon, but where the race of various parties is "mentioned"

---

gins, prosecutor said he didn't know why people rob each other when they "are practically neighbors; they speak Spanish, all of them").

41. Soap v. Carter, 632 F. 2d 872 (10th Cir. 1980). See also Commonwealth v. Tirado, 375 A2d 336 (Penn.1977) (prosecutor elicited "expert testimony" as to social values of Puerto Rican males, their honor system, and the importance of saving face in a confrontation).s

42. People v. Dukett, 308 NE 2d 590 (Ill.), cert. den 419 U.S. 965 (1974). See also Herring v. State, 522 SO 2d 745 (Miss. 1988) (prosecutor asked whether black members of the jury could vote for a fair verdict and said that some people would say a jury with eight black people would not vote for a life sentence for a black person raping a white person); Commonwealth v. Morgan, 401 A2d 1182 (Penn. 1979) (prosecutor questioned whether it was likely that a white woman would have patronized a predominantly black bar, as the defendant had claimed).

without any apparent reason for doing so. (Of course, racial images may be dredged up even when race is relevant, as it is in a description of the perpetrator of a crime, or when the behavior of some person has a racial motive.[43]) Some of these references are clearly racial, but their meaning is unclear.[44] Others look quite innocuous. For example, in one case the prosecutor made reference in his opening statement to the victim, "a young black male."[45] More disturbing is the reference to the defendant as "a black kid from Detroit."[46] Knowledge of the context (often not provided by appellate court opinions)[47] can render a single reference very disturbing. A powerful, albeit unspecified, racial content is carried by the sentence "Can you imagine her state of mind when she woke up at 6 o'clock that morning, staring into the muzzle of a gun held by this black man?"[48] Even passing references to the defendant's Colombian nationality in a narcotics case is likely to be harmful.[49] And naturally, repeated references to the race of the victim or defendant are more provocative than would be a single reference.[50]

---

43. See e.g. Commonwealth v. Washington, 28 Mass App. Ct. 271, 549 N.E. 2d 446 (1990)(explaining victim's failure to report crime to persons with whom she had contact immediately after crime had occurred as due to those persons being black the victim being afraid of black people).

44. For example, in State v. Brown, 636 SW 2d 929 (Mo.1982), cert. den., 459 U.S. 1212, the prosecutor argued that judges, reporters, prosecutors and police officers could all do their jobs"...til we're black in the face. Unless you do your job..." their efforts would be useless.." Given a black defendant and a white victim, it seems unlikely that the substitution of "black" for "blue" in the colloquial expression is nonracial, but the meaning of the substitution is uncertain. See also People v. Springs, 300 N.W. 2d 315 (Mich. 1980) (prosecutor asked what the race of defendant's prior trial counsel was).

45. State v. King, 573 So.2d 604 La. 1991).

46. Sanders v. State, 428 NE 2d 23 (Ind. 1981).

47. For an extreme example of lack of context, see People v. Dupree, 110 App Div. 2d 777 (2d Dept. 1985), 487 N.Y.S.2d 847 (holding defendant not deprived of a fair trial by prosecutor's improperly injecting race into the case without describing what prosecutor had said).

48. See Blair v. Armontrout, 916 F. 2d 1310, 1347 (8th Cir. 1990) (Heany, J., dissenting).

49. See United States v. Yonn, 702 F. 2d 1341 (11th Cir. 1983) (prosecutor and defense attorney refer to defendant's Colombian nationality in narcotics prosecution);United States v. Cardenas, 778 F2d 1127 (5th Cir. 1985);United States v. Chase, 838 F 2d 743, (5th Cir. 1988) cert. den. 108 S.Ct. 2022).

50. See e.g., Commonwealth v. Johnson, 361 N.E. 2d 212,219 (Mass. 1977) (repeated references to race of black defendant, white victim, and scene of a "project" with a heavy black population); State v. Granberry, 530 SW 2d 714 (Mo.App. 1975) (repeated reference to defendants race); Griffin V. Wainwright, 760 F.2d 1505, reh. den., enbanc (11th Cir. 1985) (five references to victims of black defendant as "white male boy," "white boy," or "white males").

Blatant and Subtle Racial Imagery

The commentary on prosecutorial misconduct tends to dismiss blatant racial appeals as a relic of a racist past, rarely to be encountered in the present (Gershman 1985; Merrill 1984; Alshuler 1972). Whether or not that comfortable perspective is accurate depends, I suppose, on what one considers blatant and what counts as rare. In my view, most of the reported cases concern blatant appeals to race, although reviewing courts have not always seen it that way. As the examples quoted at the beginning of this article and in the preceding section demonstrate, obvious appeals to racial prejudice can still be found with regularity, if not overwhelming frequency, throughout the last 30 years. Some cases are amazing as well as appalling; in one particularly egregious case, the prosecutor's remarks included the following racially inflammatory comments:

> Why is it a black Sunday? Because these two animals decided to shoot white honkies.... They were going to shoot white honkies... They were going to go shoot white honkey. What did they mean? They meant business.... They left Oakwood Shopping Center, armed themselves, and came back to shoot whitey, to kill whitey, and that's exactly what they did.... These gentlemen had the opportunity to leave at any time, at any time. Nobody forced them into that shopping center with guns to kill whitey.... Ladies and gentlemen, do you think these two black males, or any kind of males, these two animals over here....[51]

Such a case can be deemed extreme, but cases that call upon an image of black violence and criminality, albeit only once or twice, are not. Cases in which prosecutors have overtly called upon black sexual appetite or sexual threat imagery must be deemed fairly common. I count as "blatant" the use of animal imagery in a case involving African American or Latino defendants.

If reported prosecutorial misconduct cases are the visible tip of the iceberg of blatant use of racial imagery, then subtle uses of racial imagery are the unexplored Antarctica. Few of the reported cases involve imagery that I would call subtle, but it would be a mistake to infer from the dearth of cases that subtle racial imagery is rarely employed in the courtroom. Rather, the predominance of blatant cases reflects the likely disposition of claims involving more subtle abuses; courts do not always reverse even bla-

---

51. Louisiana v. Wilson, 404 So. 2d 968, 969 (La. 1981).

tant cases, and virtually never reverse more subtle abuses, thus removing the incentive to litigate the less egregious cases. Indeed, even the number of appeals that *do* raise a racial imagery claim cannot be accurately ascertained due to the practice of affirming criminal defendants' appeals without an opinion.

Social science data on prejudice and communication supports the hypothesis that the unexplored continent is vast. The social science literature documenting the persistence of negative attitudes toward African Americans is overwhelming (Aleinikoff 1992, Schuman 1991, Johnson 1985); there is less data on other minority groups, but no one would claim that stereotyping has disappeared for them either (Blalock 1982, Lipton 1983, Smith and Dempsey 1983). "Dominative" racists, persons who express bigotry and hostility openly, often employing physical force, are undoubtedly fewer in number in this country than they were 50 years ago (Johnson 1985, 1027-1028). But the diminution in the ranks of the ranks of the openly racist has been neither steady nor an unmitigated blessing; not only have recent years brought an upswing in bias related violence and hate speech, but the long term trend toward fewer open racists has been paralleled by a trend toward more closet, or "aversive" racists (Johnson 1985, 1027-1028). The phenomenon of the modern aversive racist predicts frequent resort to subtle racial imagery.

Modern racists do not want to associate with persons of color, largely because of the stereotypes they still hold (van Dijk 1987, 225). A 1990 survey by the National Opinion Research Center of the University of Chicago found that more than half of all whites believe that blacks are less intelligent, less hard-working, less patriotic—and most to the point here—more violence-prone than whites (Aleinikoff 1992, 332). Also to the point here is that twenty-five percent of white Americans still approve of anti-miscegentation laws (Aleinikoff 1992, 332n.21). These and similar surveys probably underestimate the prevalence of such stereotypes because such views may be socially stigmatized, and embarrassing to report, even to a pollster (Sigall and Page 1971, Byrnes 1988). In ordinary conversation, the aversive racist recognizes a formal anti-discrimination norm that forbids open racist evaluations and conclusions.

Recognition of the anti-discrimination norm does not, however, prevent either racial derogation or racially biased decisionmaking. In a fascinating linguistic study of white conversations about minorities in the United States and Holland, Teun A. van Dijk observed a variety of recurring speech patterns (van Dijk 1987). Racial stories are generally not "I" stories, but "we" stories; group membership is signaled often by reference to group goals. It is most successful when the self can be identified as a victim, both because it is more persuasive, and because it allows the whole group to see itself as a victim, thus entitled to the negative feelings it has about a racial outgroup (van Dijk 1987, 288). The telling and hearing of these stories is thus functional for the majority, and despite the anti-discrimination norm, occurs quite frequently.

The formal norm, particularly in settings where the racial views of the audience are unknown, makes direct attribution of negative personality characteristics to a race risky, and therefore relatively rare; politeness and indirection funtion to preserve the positive presentation of self (van Dijk 1987, 87). Racist evaluations and conclusions are often toned down through various semantic moves. Negative acts are often described with the racist conclusion left implicit (van Dijk 1987, 68). Thus, it is not surprising that in the sexual threat imagery cases, the argument that "miscegenation" is wrong is not made; it is enough, and safer, to merely tell the jury about the defendant's interracial sexual activity. Examples and generalizations are also common (van Dijk 1987, 90-91); hence, the prosecutorial reminders of how much "black on black" crime there is. Again, overt arguments of racial propensity are not necessary.

Prejudiced talk often includes contrasts between the majority group and the disliked minority. Contrast, may however, be stated in very vague terms, with nonverbal cues such as pitch, intonation and facial expression conveying the opinion of the speaker about the ethnic outgroup. Prejudiced talk often utilizes pronouns of distance. "They," "them," "those people" and similar euphemisms emphasize separation while protecting the speaker from the risk of social disapproval that accompanies overt racial pronouncements (van Dijk 1987, 104). Thus, were courts inclined to regulate the more subtle forms of racially motivated microagressions by prosecutors, they would be faced with a very difficult task; unfortunately, they do not yet seem to be very active in deterring even quite blatant racial derogations.

Existing Legal Constraints on Prosecutorial Summation

Prosecutors are theoretically constrained in summation by statutory requirements that prohibit arguing facts not in the record and appealing to the prejudice of jurors as well as by the Due Process Clause of the Fourteenth Amendment. Often it is unclear whether the "fundamental fairness" the court is assessing stems from the due process clause, or some other source, and it rarely matters.

What is most striking is the large number of convictions that appellate courts have affirmed despite the prosecutor's use of racial imagery in her summation. There is a passel of reasons for the court's refusal to reverse these convictions. First come the cases in which the trial judge's instruction to disregard the prosecutor's comments is deemed to have cured the error,[52] as though racial prejudice can only be stirred up with the judge's permission. Even more surprisingly, inferences from the jury's observable behavior have been sufficient assurance that the verdict need not be reversed. In one instance the appellate court relied upon the trial court's purported observation of adverse reaction by the jury to the prosecutor's racial argument;[53] in another, upon the jury's request to review testimony and receive additional instructions.[54] Again, a false supposition underlies these cases. This time it is a misunderstanding of modern racism; a jury may disapprove of openly racist statements and it may rationally attempt to balance the evidence, but that only indicates that the jurors are not overtly racist, and not that they may not be influenced by racial imagery (Devine 1989).

Another common reason for failing to reverse for racial imagery is that the defendant or her counsel invited or sanctioned the imagery.[55] Some of these cases involve real stretching. For example, in one case, the fact that the defense attorney had made references to the complaining witness in a rape case as a "white woman" or "white lady" was said to have invited the prosecutor's argument that if jury believed the complainant, they would have to believe that the black defendant "...took it, he got him a white woman."[56] More broadly, the problem with relying on defense counsel "invitations" in this area ignores that defense counsel too may be racist, that references to race not intended to provoke prejudice may nevertheless do so, and that references to race may be cumulative in their impact.

Then there are the cases that rely upon defense counsel's lack of objection to sustain the conviction. Most courts require a higher level of improper conduct, sometimes called "plain error," before reversing a case where the defendant's lawyer did not object to the prosecutor's misconduct; such a two tier standard is not peculiar to these cases. The idea is that the error should be so apparent, so "plain" that a trial judge would know it was wrong even without an objection by defense counsel, and should on his own do something to correct it. What is a surprise, then, is not the requirement of plain error, but the egregious remarks courts have considered minor enough misconduct that it does not rise to the level of "plain error."

---

52. People v. Dupree, 487 N.Y.S. 2d 847, 849 (App.Div. 1985); People v. Flores, (Ill. 1979); United States v. Pena, 793 F.2d 486 (2d Cir. 1986); Herring v. State 522 So2d 745 (Miss. 1988);Nquyen v. State, 547 So2d. 582 (Ala. 1988.);State v. Martinez, 658 P2d 428 (N.M. 1983) .

53. People v. Dukett, 308 NE2d 590 (Ill. 1974).

54. People v. Rivera, 426 N.Y.S. 2d 785 (App. Div. 1980).

55. See e.g., Commonwealth v. Lopez, 530 NE2d. 1247 (Mass. 1988); U.S. v. Cardenas, 778 F2d 1127 (5th Cir 1985); United States v. Yonn, 702 F2d 1341 (11th Cir. 1983); Rhoden v. State, 274 So 2d 630 (Ala. 1973) .

56. Rhoden v. State, 274 So 2d 630 (Ala. 1973).

The following have been held to *not* be plain error: characterizing a black defendant with the obvious racial epithet;[57] falsely attributing the epithet "honkey" to a black defendant;[58] arguing that the defendant's Middle East background made him more likely to be greedy;[59] arguing that "no person in their right mind would want to remember three black men getting on her naked body";[60] arguing that it was not believable that the defendant had not entered the robbed premises because it was incredible that the co-defendant would leave "a black guy out there in a car…while a robbery was going on…";[61] arguing that because a white woman had lived with a black man for two years, she had already faced a lot of social disapproval and therefore would be more likely to lie for him;[62] and questioning, "Can you imagine her state of mind when she woke up at 6 o'clock that morning, staring into the muzzle of a gun held by this black man?"[63] Apparently trial judges cannot be expected to know that these remarks are improper!

The next obstacle to reversal is the "harmless error" doctrine. Like the plain error doctrine, harmless error analysis is common in a wide variety of cases. The theory is that even when something improper or unconstitutional has occurred during the course of a trial, there is no reason to hold a new trial if the reviewing court is convinced that the error was harmless (i.e., would not have affected the outcome). While one court has held that harmless error doctrine does not apply to racially inflammatory summations,[64] most courts do not make such an exception. Upon finding overwhelming evidence of guilt, courts usually affirm the conviction despite remarks they deem patently improper on the supposition that any error is harmless. The problem with this reasoning, however is twofold: first, given the power of racial stereotypes, it is difficult to know how they may have affected a verdict, particularly a death sentence; and second, absent reversals, a prosecutor has no incentive to change his or her conduct in the future. As Georges-Abeyie points out, the fact that we do not have official or precise measures of the effects of racist remarks does not diminish the severity of their effects (Georges-Abeyie 1987), but it does permit the proliferation of such remarks.

---

57. Thornton v. Beto, 470 F2d 657 (5th Cir 1972).
58. U.S. v. Harvey, 756 F2d 636 (1985).
59. People v. Marij, 180 Mich App 525, 447 N.W.2d 835 (1989).
60. State v. Mayhue, 653 So2d 227 (Mo 1983).
61. State v. Snowden, 675 P2d 289 (Ariz. 1983).
62. State v. Terry, 582 S.W. 2d 337 (Mo. 1979).
63. Blair v. Armontrout, 916 F 2d 1310,1347 (8th Cir. 1990) (Henaey, J., concurring and dissenting).
64. Weddington v. State, 545 A.2d 607 (Del. 1988). See also, Haynes v. McKendrick, 481 F2d (2d Cir. 1973) (suggesting harmless error doctrine may not apply to verdicts tainted by racial prejudice; Miller v. N.C., 583 F2d 701 (4th Cir. 1978) (same).

After the procedural hurdles to reversal come a variety of reasons relating to the content of what was said. Probably the most frequent reason for minimizing—or taking seriously—the offense is a reference to the prosecutor's supposed intent. It was not "race-baiting" to ask the jury to imagine the fear of the victim as a prisoner of three black strangers;[65] the repeated references black defendants, white victims, and the black "projects" where the crime took place were not racially motivated, but just "amateur psychologizing."[66] Similarly, it was not misconduct to refer to black prison gangs to rehabilitate a white witness where the prosecutor could have reasonably believed that the asserted attacks were relevant to the witness' fear of retaliation if he testified against the defendant.[67] Most revolting is a Utah court's pronouncement that while "we express no opinion on the soundness of the proposition that casual sexual encounters between people of different races are less likely than between people of the same race," as the prosecutor implied, "there is no indication that the remark was made with derogatory intent or to imply that because the defendant was black, he was more likely to have committed the alleged crime."[68] Why the prosecutor's motives should matter at all in these cases is unclear, since the question is not her purity but the trial's fairness. Even if motive should matter, one would think that racist motives encompass more than unsophisitcated, unfashionable straightforward racial animosity. Indeed, the very fact that courts find some of these arguments plausible suggests a greater danger that jurors will find them persuasive; it does not alter their racial character.

A more drastic minimizing device is to declare that some remarks have no racial content.[69] Thus in one case with a black defendant and three separate prosecutorial references to animals (that jurors should not "digress to where the animals are," that they should rise above "animalistic intolerance," that the defendants had treated the victim's girlfriend "like an animal"), the court said that it could not say the remarks were racially prejudical, given that the defendants were not *referred to* as animals.[70] Perhap

65. Russell v. Collins, 944 F.2d 202 (5th Cir. 1991).

66. Commonwealth v. Johnson, 361 NE.2d 212,219 (Mass. 1977).

67. People v. Malone, 762 P2d. 1249 (Cal.), cert den. 490 US 1095.

68. State v. Thomas, 777 P2d 445 (Utah 1989).

69. There are enough of these cases that I am persuaded that the approach suggested by Earle, supra note 1, at least without amploification, is unworkable. She argues that explicit references to race and indirect referecnes, as judged by a "reasonable person" standard should be considered prosecutorial racism. There is so much resistance to seeing the racial content of remarks that judges who think of themselves as reasonable people will not necessarily identify racial overtones. At least an illustrative list is necessary. (See above.)

70.State v. Lombard 471 So2d 782, (La. App 5th Cir 1985), aff'd in part and rev'd in part on other grounds, 486 So 2d 106.

most amazing is the escalating denial evident in the following explanation of a prosecutor's various comments:

> [The defendant] claims the State's final argument was calculated to inflame the passions of the jury through appeals to racial prejudice. [He] proposes the comment that [the codefendant] was "stuck, by his own stupidity" in a bedroom is an "indirect, but unmistakable reference to the race of the Defendants." He makes the same charges regarding a reference to the persons who simply carry out orders as "these privates" and the group of persons as "the boys." These terms are used as general slang, and not racial comment. [The defendant] professes to see a racial reference to the remark "this one and that one..." These remarks are not inherently racial comments. Two other phrases are discussed by [the defendant]. First, the prosecutor characterized the testimony of a black defense witness as "shucking and jiving on the stand." The term is clearly of black origin, used to mean to talk in a patently misleading or evasive manner. Its use reminds the jury of the untrustworthy appearance of this witness. Second, the prosecutor said [the defendant] "had to play Superfly" and shoot [the victim] where he lay. Despite the racial content of the term "Superfly," it is not out of bounds to make such an allusion by saying [the defendant] acted like "Superfly," either to characterize his actions by comparison with a known fictional figure, or to imply that [his] behavior is to some extent modeled on the fictional figure.[71]

This opinions make the reader wonder again if the only forbidden arguments are the ridiculously direct arguments from race (e.g., "We know he did it because he is black"), the kind of argument the norm of formal equality suggests would rarely be risked.

Even when racial content is acknowledged—as sometimes it really must be—courts may deprecate its significance. It is not uncommon for a court to deem the reference to race as isolated or not thematic.[72] Sometimes a

71. Smith v. State 516 NE 2d 1055,1064 (Ind. 1987).

72. State v. Ali, 551 N.Y.S. 2d 54 (2d Dept. 1990) (testimony of witnesses and one remark by prosecutor on race of police officers and informant); US v. Abello-Silva, 948 F2d 1168 (10th Cir 1991) (defendant "secure in the comfort of Colombian corruption..laughs at American justice" and defendant is "biggest fish landed by U.S. out of that Colombian sea of narcotics", where trial of several weeks and closing argument of several hours, and statements were factually supported by the evidence); Russell v. State, 518 A2d 1081 (Md. 1987) (reference to Jamaican drug trafficking in opening statement) : People v. Traylor, 487 NE 2d 1040 (Ill.1985) (being a "white policeman in a black neighborhood" explains behavior of officers);People v. Bramlett,, 569 NE. 2d 1139 (Ill.1991) (twice argued that officer should be believed because both he and the accused were, and cross-examined in defendant as to why

court minimizes not the number, but the invidiousness of the remark.[73] Thus, for example, several cases comment that remarks about sex between black men and white women are not prejudicial, or at least not very prejudicial because the jurors could see that the defendant was black and the victim white.[74] Also disheartening is a Michigan court's conclusion that a "limited number" of references to the defendant and his companion as "colored" *were not made in a derogatory manner*" and would not have diverted jury.[75]

Most surprising of all are some of the racial arguments that courts find entirely proper, such as the argument that a witness, because she was the daughter of dentist and a religious person, would not go out with person not of her race. One court postulated that the prosecutor's statement "it's hard for me to tell people of the Negro race apart" was proper to explain the complaining witness's doubts regarding the identity of one of the defendants;[76] apparently the relevance of this argument is that the jury should convict despite the witness' uncertainty!

All of uncensored pleas for so-called "equal enforcement" error[77] seem naive to me, given the conventions of modern racist speech, but one is particularly egregious: In a case in which the prosecutor urged the jury not to be hard on the defendant just because he was black and the child victim of his sexual offense was white, the reviewing court found no indication of his "lack of sincerity" and no error.[78]

---

another black person would accuse him); People v. Johnson 499 NE 2d 1355 (Ill. 1986) ("that black man"); State v. Thomas, 777 P2d 445 (Utah 1989) (argument that white victim was less likely to consent to sex with defendant because he was black).

73. See e.g. State v. Kamel, 466 NE2d 860 (argument that witnesses were unreliable due to being defendant's countrymen, and also by reason of their foreign birth not so prejudicial as to deny them a fair trial); Commonwealth v. Askins, 18 Mass App 927, 465 NE2d 1224 (1984) (reference to "foreign accent" of physician witness for defendant, "if intended as a racial slur," did not approach in emphasis or relevance, reversible error).

74. State v. Mayhue, 653 SW 2d 227 (Mo. 1983); State v. Thomas, 777 P2d 445 (Utah 1989); State v. Rhoden v. State, 274 So2d 630(1973). See also, People v. Nichols, 308 NE 2d 848 (5th Dist. 1974) (prosecutor's reference to black defendant being married to a white woman not so prejudicial where already established in the testimony and wife had appeared as a witness).

75. People v. Wilson, 198 NW 2d 424 (1972)See also, Commonwealth v. Morgan, 401 A2d 1182 (Penn. 1979) (prosecutor's argument that white girl would not have patronized a black bar was poorly stated and to a degree improper, but did not constitute misconduct that subverted due process.)

76. Patterson v. Commonwealth, 555 SW 2d 607 (Ky App 1977).

77. State v. Lee, 631 S.W.2d 453 (Tenn 1982); Clark v. State, 692 S.W.2d 203 (Tex. 1985); Wilder v. State, 401 So. 2d 151 (Ala. 1981);State v. Stamps, 569 S.W. 2d 762 (Mo 1978).

78. Dixon v. Commonwealth, 487 S.W. 2d 928 (Ky 1972).

Giving a Nod

Thus the protections for minority race defendants against the use of racial imagery to enhance the likelihood of their conviction are woefully inadequate. If we care enough about the perpetuation of racial stereotypy, if we care enough about the way such stereotypy degrades the person stereotyped and the criminal process, we will do something. Disagreement should be limited to the question of what.

Making a gesture is not nothing. It can be cheap; it can be a first step; even a nod acknowledges existence. The very least we might do, as lawyers, is to incorporate a provision forbidding the use of racial imagery by prosecutors into the professional code of ethics. The provision ought to specifically refer to (1) all unnecessary references to race or ethnicity, (2) all insinuations that a person's race or ethnicity made her more or less likely to make a choice in a given way,[79] and (3)all depictions of persons as less worthy of respect than other human beings because of their race or ethnicity. More generally, any other use of language or inflection or gesture that deliberately calls on or unnecessarily emphasizes supposed differences between racial or ethnic groups should be forbidden.

Would the practical effect of ethical constraints in this area be so small that efforts in this direction are pointless? No. It would be a step forward, albeit a small one, to acknowledge that this is a problem common enough to merit its own ethical canon, and not a remnant of a racist past so aberrational that it can be relegated to a generality prohibiting "inflammatory" argument.

Giving a Rip

But why should we not do more? What would justify having a rape shield law but not a racial imagery shield law? Reform was warranted in rape prosecutions, because "good woman"/"bad woman" imagery threatened accuracy, because it rendered the victim's experience in court humiliating, because the prospect of such humiliation discouraged complaints,

---

79. This phrasing is intended to permit argument that the evidence shows racial motive on the part of this particular defendant; it is also intended to permit arguments based not upon choice, but upon inability. Thus argument for the statistically supported proposition that a white witness is more likely to be mistaken about the identity of a black person would be permitted whereas argument that she was more likely to be lying about her belief that the accused was the perpetrator would not.

and because awareness that the rape of a "bad woman" would probably go unpunished may have encouraged some rapes. Racial imagery presents obvious analogs to each of these dangers, and adds one more: the possibility of convicting the factually innocent. Moreover, there is the additional force of constitutional command: governmental uses for race ordinarily require that the classification be necessary to the accomplishment of a compelling governmental interest. If we know adherence to that standard is sporadic at best, then surely the Fourteenth Amendment's Equal Protection Clause bolsters, if it does not command, a prophylactic statute.

In order to be effective, we would need to start with a broad definition. Here is my attempt:

> "Racial imagery" is any word, metaphor, argument, comment, gesture, or intonation that suggests, either explicitly or through commonly understood allusion, that
>
> (1) a person's race or ethnicity affects his or her standing as a full, capable, and decent human being; or
>
> (2) a person's race or ethnicity in any way affects the credibility of that person's assertions; or
>
> (3) a person's race or ethnicity in any way affects the likelihood that he or she would choose a particular course of conduct, whether criminal or noncriminal; or
>
> (4) a persons race or ethnicity in any way affects the appropriate sanctions for a crime committed by or against him or her; or
>
> (5) a person's race or ethnicity sets him or her apart from members of the jury, or makes him or her allied with members of the jury, or more generally, that a person's race or ethnicity allies him or her with other persons of the same race or ethnic group or separates him or her from persons of the same race or ethnic group.
>
> (6) Racial imagery will be conclusively presumed from the unnecessary use of a racially descriptive word.
>
> (7) Where a metaphor or simile uses the word "white," "black," "brown," "yellow" or "red"; where any comparisons to animals of any kind are made; or where characters, real or fictional, who are strongly identified with a racial or ethnic group are referred to, racial imagery will be presumed, subject only to rebuttal through proof that the term in question could not have racial connotations with respect to any witness, defendant, attorney, or judge involved in the case.
>
> (8) That a prosecutor disclaims racial intent, either contemporaneously or at a later date, shall have no bearing upon the determination of whether his or her remarks or actions constitute a use of racial imagery.

Such a broad definition will require some exceptions, and it may be that an adequate list of exceptions requires more heads than one. But I would start with the assumption that any prosecutorial use of racial imagery should be subject to the strict scrutiny standard.[80] Assuming that discerning the truth in a criminal prosecution is a compelling governmental interest, any use of racial imagery should be *necessary* to the discernment of the truth. At the least, that would seem to require that the probative value of the imagery clearly outweigh the risk of prejudice; I would suppose that it also requires that the probative value of the evidence could not be captured in a way that did not implicate race, or implicated race to a lesser extent. I would therefore begin with only two exceptions to the use of racial imagery by a prosecutor in closing argument: first, where a racial motive is alleged for the offense *and* there is direct evidence that the defendant entertained a racial motive *and* that motive is argued in terms that are not unnecessarily inflammatory; and second, where racial animosity is alleged to have motivated a witness to lie *and* there is a good faith basis for that allegation *and* that motive is argued in terms that are not unnecessarily inflammatory. I am convinced that something very close to an automatic reversal standard is necessary.[81] The urge to affirm convictions of "obviously" guilty defendants is so strong, the pattern of finding a reason to affirm in these cases so thoroughly entrenched, that I know of no other way to assure each defendant that his trial was not unnecessarily tainted by racial prejudice. This position assumes that "taint" occurs not only when the result is altered, but when race is injected into (or, perhaps more commonly, underlined during) the process. The Delaware Supreme Court has so held, reasoning that "the right to a fair trial that is free of racial implications is so basic to the federal Constitution that an infringement upon that right can never be treated as harmless error."[82]

Such a statute would affect many trials. Undoubtedly prosecutors would become more cautious in preparing their summations, and in a vast number of anonymous cases, the courtroom participants would be spared the

---

80. The only two cases of which I am aware that applies this standard are McFarland v. Smith, 611 F. 2d 414 (2d Cir. 1979) and Weddington v. State, 545 A. 2d 607(Del. 1988).

81. The one exception that strikes me as worth considering is a single, descriptive, neutral, but unnecessary reference to race in a context that is not inflammatory. Describing the victim as "a young black male" would fall into that category. Describing the victim as "a nice white lady" would not; asking "Can you imagine her state of mind when she woke up at 6 o'clock that morning, staring into the muzzle of a gun held by this black man?" would not. Cf. DeBrota, supra note 1 (advocating an exception to the harmless error for prosecutor has appealed to racial prejudice of jury, but discussing only egregious cases.)

82. Weddington v. State, 545 A. 2d 607 (Del. 1988).

ten thousandth dose of poison. One small corner of the our nation's discourse would be both lighter and darker; whatever those words mean elsewhere, *I* mean: both more illuminating and closer to the truth.

Giving When It Hurts

A racial imagery shield law would not be enough. It is hard to imagine what could be enough to root out racial imagery from jury deliberations. In the end, the shield law might prevent the reinforcement of biases, the focusing of blurred images, the reconfiguration of old stereotypes, but it could never erase the reels and reels of racial films viewed over a lifetime. Nothing can do that. Why is darkness a thing of dread? Maybe our ancestors feared the dark for the predators they could not see. But darkness is also the womb, the bed, the shade; why don't those "realities" find metaphors in our speech? Can white people see those realities? If they could see them, how could white prosecutors say all the things they have said?

It pains white people to admit that they are not the standard, the neutral baseline decision maker against which others should be compared. It pains (not only white people, but all those who need and want to believe in ultimate fairness) to acknowledge that the typical decision maker is not the ideal decision maker, that racial prejudice is not an aberration, that it taints everyone it touches, and that it touches everyone. It is one thing to say that a lawyer may not strike a juror because of his or her race; we admit only that a minority race juror in a case with a minority defendant is not presumptively *less* competent, *less* fair than the white juror. What is hard for white people to admit is that the minority race juror is *more* likely to be competent, *more* likely to be fair. The cost of not acknowledging the inadequacies of white decision makers, however, is not merely psychological discomfort; it is wrongful convictions for innocent defendants, as well as wrongful not-so-"petit" indignities for guilty defendants, jurors, lawyers, judges, and the observing public. Moreover, these costs fall, as Georges-Abeyie predicts, almost exclusively on people of color (Georges-Abeyie 1987).

Of course people of color have seen the same films, heard the same metaphors, lived with the same torrent of images of white as pure, good, light, clean, true, safe, normal, right—and the contrasting flood of negative images of blackness, brownness, yellowness, redness, "nonwhiteness." But at least most of them have other images too. At least there is also the lived warmth of color, the contrary images, and the lived pain of the distorting images.

This is not a matter of speculation. If the entire body of relevant data is surveyed, the inference that race influences the white jurors' determination of guilt is unavoidable. As I have argued at great length elsewhere, taking together the observations and statistics from criminal trials, the results of mock jury experiments, and conclusions from general research on racial prejudice, it is clear that justice would be advanced by greater minority participation in juries (Johnson 1985). A survey of the breadth and frequency of the criminal trial uses of racial imagery provides one more reason for mandatory inclusion of minority jurors, at least in cases with minority defendants; we cannot eradicate the imagery, but we can give voice to richer perspectives on that imagery.

References

Adler, Patricia. 1993. *Wheeling and Dealing*. New York: Columbia University Press.

Aleinikoff, Alexander. 1992. The Constitution in Context: The Continuing Significance of Racism. *Colorado Law Review* 63: 325.

Alschuler, Albert W. 1972. Courtroom Misconduct by Prosecutors and Trial Judges. *Texas Law Review* 50: 629.

Anderson, Elijah. 1994. The Code of the Streets. *Atlantic Monthly* (August): 82.

Arizona Criminal and Traffic Law Manual. 1994. Charlottesville, VA: The Michie Company.

Arizona Republic. 2000. Feds Investigate Police Beating Philadelphia Arrest on Videotape. 14 July.

Bachman, Jerald, Katherine Wadsworth, Patrick O'Malley, Lloyd Johnston, and John Schulenberg. 1997. *Smoking, Drinking and Drug Use in Young Adulthood: The Impacts of New Freedoms and New Responsibilities*. Mahwah, NJ: Lawrence Erlbaum.

Baldus, David, and George Woodworth. 1998. Race Discrimination and the Death Penalty: An Empirical and Legal Overview. In *America's Experiment with Capital Punishment*, edited by James Acker, Robert Bohm, and Charles Lanier. Durham, NC: Carolina Academic Press.

Baldwin, James. 1961. *Nobody Knows My Name: More Notes of a Native Son*. New York: The Dial Press.

Barker, Elizabeth. 1996. Car Clubs To Protest Cruising Ban. *The Arizona Republic* 26 May: B1, B4.

Beck, Melinda. 1995. Enforcing Teen Curfews. *Newsweek* 17 July: 53.

Belenko, Steven. 1993. *Crack and the Evolution of Anti-Drug Policy*. Westport, CT: Greenwood.

Bell, Derrick, Jr. 1992. *Faces at the Bottom of the Well: The Permanence of Racism*. New York: Basic Books.

Bertram, Eva, Morris Blachman, Kenneth Sharpe, and Peter Andreas. 1996. *Drug War Politics*. Berkeley: University of California Press.

Biskupic, Joan. 1999. In Jury Rooms, a Form of Civil Protest Grows. *The Washington Post* 8 February.

Black, Donald. 1989. *Sociological Justice*. New York: Oxford University Press.

Blalock, Herbert, Jr. 1982. *Race and Ethnic Relations*. Englewood Cliffs, NJ: Prentice-Hall.

Blumstein, Alfred. 1993. Racial Disproportionality of U.S. Prison Populations Revisited. *University of Colorado Law Review* 64: 743.

Brest, Paul. 1976. The Supreme Court, 1975 Term. *Harvard Law Review* 90: 1.

Brewer, Marilyn B. 1988. A Dual Process Model of Impressions Formation. In *Advances in Social Cognition*.

Bright, Brenda Jo. 1995. Remappings: Los Angeles Low Riders. In Bright and Bakewell 1995.

Bright, Brenda Jo, and Liza Bakewell, eds. 1995. *Looking High and Low: Art and Cultural Identity*. Tucson: University of Arizona Press.

Bunch, Lonnie, III. 1990. A Past Not Necessarily Prologue: The Afro-American in Los Angeles Since 1900. In *20th Century Los Angeles: Power, Promotion, and Social Conflict*, edited by Norman Klein and Martin Schiesl. Claremont: Regina Books.

Bureau of Justice Statistics. 1997. *One in Five U.S. Residents in Contact with Police During Year*. Washington, D.C.: U.S. Department of Justice.

———. 1998a. *Criminal Offenders Statistics*. Washington, DC: U.S. Department of Justice.

———. 1998b. *Homicide trends in the United States*. Washington, D.C.: U.S. Department of Justice.

———. 2000a. *Federal Law Enforcement Statistics*. Washington, D.C.: U.S. Department of Justice.

———. 2000b. *Local Police Departments, 1997*. Washington D.C.: U.S. Department of Justice.

Butler, Paul. 1995. Racially Based Jury Nullification: Black Power in the Criminal Justice System. *Yale Law Journal* 105: 677-692.

Byrnes, Deborah A. 1988. Contemporary Measures of Attitudes toward Blacks. *Education & Psychology Measurement* 48: 107.

Carter, Kathy Barrett. 1999. Profiling Ruling Haunts Officials. *Star Ledger* 21 March: 21, 27.

Center for Research on Criminal Justice. 1977. *The Iron Fist and the Velvet Glove: An Analysis of the U.S. Police*. Berkeley: Center for Research on Criminal Justice.

Childs, John Brown. 1997. The New Youth Peace Movement. *Social Justice* 24(4): 247-257.

Chivers, C.J. 1999. Ex-Police Leader's Claim of Bias Attacked. In *New York Times* 4 October.

Clayton, Richard. 1995. *Marihuana in the "Third World": Appalachia, USA.* Boulder, CO: Lynne Rienner.

Cole, David. 1999. *No Equal Justice: Race and Class in the American Criminal Justice System.* New York: The New Press.

Collins, Patricia. 1993. Toward a New Vision: Race, Class, and Gender as Categories of Analysis and Connections. *Race, Sex, Class* 1(1): 3.

Connell, Rich, and Robert J. Lopez. 1999. Rampart Probe May Put Gang Injunction at Risk. *Los Angeles Times* September 19: A1, A21, A22.

Cooper, Martha, and Joseph Sciorra. 1994. *R.I.P.: Memorial Wall Art.* New York: Henry Holt.

Cornell, Drucilla. 1999. *Beyond Accommodation: Ethical, Feminism, Deconstruction, and the Law.* New York: Rowman and Littlefield.

Covington, Jeanette. 1991. The Black Community and the War on Drugs. In *Blacks in New Jersey: Crime, Drugs, Justice and African Americans.* Eleventh Annual Report of the New Jersey Public Policy Research Institute. Newark, NJ: New Jersey Public Policy Research Institute.

———. 1997. The Social Construction of the Minority Drug Problem. *Social Justice* 24(4): 117.

Cox, Dick. 1998. Curfews: Benefit or Bad News? *Law and Order* 46(12): 87.

Crenshaw, Kimberle. 1989. Demarginalizing the Intersections of Race and Sex: A Black Feminist Critique of Antidiscrimination Doctrine. *University of Chicago Legal Forum* 139-167.

———. 1993. Beyond Racism and Misogyny: Black Feminism and 2 Live Crew. In Matsuda et al. 1993.

Daly, Kathleen. 1994. Criminal Law and Justice System Practices as Racist, White, and Racialized. *Washington & Lee Law Review* 51: 431-32.

Davis, Peggy. 1989. Law as Microaggression. *Yale Law Journal* 98: 1559.

Davis, Robert and Arthur Lurigio 1996. *Fighting Back: Neighborhood Antidrug Strategies.* Thousand Oaks, CA: Sage.

Daza, Rosario. 1996. Police Defend Number of Hispanics Picked up on Curfew Violations. *The Arizona Republic* 11 August: B4.

DeBrota, Steven D. 1989. Arguments Appealing to Racial Prejudice: Uncertainty, Impartiality and the Harmless Error Doctrine. *Indiana Law Journal* 64: 375.

Devine, Patricia G. 1989. Stereotypes and Prejudice: Their Automatic and Controlled Components. *Journal of Personality & Social Psychology* 56: 5.

DiIulio, John. 1996. My Black Crime Problem, and Ours. *City Journal* 6: 14.

Donohue, John. 1999a. Expert witness testimony in the case *ACLU v. State of Illinois.*

———. 1999b. Boss Warns Troopers: Don't Target Minorities. *Star Ledger* 28 February: 1.

Earle, Elizabeth E. 1992. Note. *Columbia Law Review* 92: 1212.

Ewick, Patricia, and Susan Silbey. 1998. *The Common Place of Law.* Chicago: University Press.

Ferrell, Jeff. 1995. Urban Graffiti: Crime, Control, and Resistance. *Youth and Society* 27(1): 73-92.

———. 1996. *Crimes of Style: Urban Graffiti and the Politics of Criminality.* Boston: Northeastern University Press.

———. 1997. Youth, Crime and Cultural Space. *Social Justice* 24(4): 21-38.

———. 1998. Freight Train Graffiti: Subculture, Crime, Dislocation. *Justice Quarterly* 15(4): 587-608.

———. 1999a. Cultural Criminology. *Annual Review of Sociology* 25: 395-418.

———. 1999b. Author Interview with Caycee Cullen. Berkeley, California (August 6).

———. 2001. *Tearing Down the Streets.* New York: St. Martin's.

Ferrell, Jeff, and Clinton R. Sanders, eds. 1995. *Cultural Criminology.* Boston: Northeastern University Press.

Ferrell, Jeff, and Neil Websdale, eds. 1999. *Making Trouble: Cultural Constructions of Crime, Deviance, and Control.* New York: Aldine de Gruyter.

Fiscus, Chris. 1998. Phoenix Aims to Break Gangs' Grip. *The Arizona Republic* 23 May: A1, 2.

Fiscus, Chris, and Pat Kossan. 1996. Slaying Pours Fuel on Cruising Bonfire. *The Arizona Republic* 30 April: A1, A8.

Foucault, Michel. 1995. *Discipline and Punish.* New York: Vintage.

Georges-Abeyie, Daniel. 1981. Studying Black Crime: A Realistic Approach. In *Environmental Criminology*, edited by P.J. Brantingham and P. L. Brantingham. Thousand Oaks, CA: Sage.

———, ed. 1984. *The Criminal Justice System and Blacks.* New York: C. Boardman, Co.

———. 1989. Race, Ethnicity and the Spatial Dynamic: Toward a Realistic Study of Black Crime, Crime Victimization and Criminal Justice Processing of Blacks. *Social Justice* 16(4): 35.

———. 1990a. The Myth of a Racist Criminal Justice System? In MacLean and Milovanovic 1990.

———. 1990b. Criminal Justice Processing of Non-White Minorities. In MacLean and Milovanovic 1990.

———. 1992. Defining Race, Ethnicity, and Social Distance: Their Impact on Crime, Criminal Victimization, and the Criminal Justice Processing of Minorities. *Journal of Contemporary Criminal Justice* 8(2):100.

Gershman, Bennet L. 1985. *Prosecutorial Misconduct.* New York: C. Boardman and Co.

Glaser, Barney, and Anselm Strauss. 1967. *The Discovery of Grounded Theory.* Chicago: Aldine.

Goffman, Erving. 1973. *The Presentation of Self in Everyday Life.* New York: The Overlook Press.

Goldberg, Jeffrey. 1999. The Color of Suspicion. *New York Times Magazine* 20 June: 50-57, 64, 85, 87.

Green, Lorraine. 1996. *Policing Places With Drug Problems.* Thousand Oaks, CA: Sage.

Greene, Judith. 1999. Zero Tolerance: A Case Study of Police Policies and Practices in New York City. *Crime and Delinquency* 45(2).

Greenhouse, Linda. 1999. Loitering Law Aimed at Gangs Is Struck Down By High Court." *New York Times* 11 June: A1.

———. 2000. Flight Can Justify Search by the Police, High Court Rules. *New York Times* 13 January: A1.

Gurnon, Emily. 1999. Turf War Targets "Yuppies" in SF. *The Arizona Republic* 19 June 19: A26.

Hagedorn, John M. 1990. Back in the Field Again: Gang Research in the Nineties. *Gangs in America*, edited by C. Ronald Huff. Newbury Park, CA: Sage.

Harcourt, Bernard. 1998. Reflecting on the Subject: A Critique of the Social Influence Conception of Deterrence, the Broken Windows Theory, and Order Maintenance Policing New York Style. *Michigan Law Review* 97: 291.

Harker, Victoria. 1999. Action to Curb Gang Targets Area, Residents Claim. *The Arizona Republic* 22 October: B5

Harris, David. 1999a. *Driving While Black: Racial Profiling on Our Nation's Highways.* American Civil Liberties Union Special Report. New York: ACLU.

———. 1999b. The Stories, the Statistics, and the Law: Why "Driving While Black" Matters. *Minnesota Law Review* 84(2): 265-326.

Henry, Stuart, and Dragan Milovanovic. 1996. *Constitutive Criminology.* London: Sage.

Herbert, Steve. 1997. *Policing Space: Territoriality and the Los Angeles Police Department.* Minneapolis: University of Minnesota Press.

Higginbotham, A. Leon, Jr. 1996. *Shades of Freedom: Racial Politics and Presumptions of The American Legal Process.* New York: Oxford University Press.

Holohan, John. 1972. The Economics of Heroin. In *Dealing with Drug Abuse: A Report to the Ford Foundation*, edited by P. Wald. New York: Praeger.

Human Rights Watch. 2000. *Punishment and Prejudice: Racial Dispari-ties in the War on Drugs.* Available on-line at http://www.hrw.org/reports/2000/usa/Rcedrg00.htm.

Innes, Martin. 1999. An Iron Fist in an Iron Glove?: The Zero Tolerance Policing Debate. *Howard Journal* 38(4).

Jacobius, Arleen. 1997. Court Approves Gang Injunctions. *ABA Journal* 83(April): 34.

Johnson, Robert, and Paul Leighton. 1995. Black Genocide? Preliminary Thoughts on the Plight of America's Poor Black Men. *Journal of African American Men,* 1(2): 3.

Johnson, Sheri Lyn. 1985. Black Innocence and the White Jury. *Michigan Law Review* 83: 1611.

Johnston, Lloyd, and Patrick O'Malley. 1997. The Recanting of Earlier Re-ported Drug Use by Young Adults. In *The Validity of Self-Reported Drug Use: Improving the Accuracy of Survey Estimates,* edited by Lana Harrison and Arthur Hughes. Rockville, MD: NIDA.

Johnston, Lloyd, Patrick O'Malley, and Jerald Bachman. 1998. *National Survey Results on Drug Use from Monitoring the Future, 1975-1997.* Volume 1. Washington, D.C.: U.S. Department of Health and Human Services.

Kantako, Konnadi, Mbanna Kantako, Jr., and Ebony Kantako. 1998. Ghetto Radio Rap Song. In *Seizing the Airwaves,* edited by Ron Sakol-sky and Stephen Dunifer. San Francisco: AK Press.

Keith, Michael. 1997. Street Sensibility? Negotiating the Political by Ar-ticulating the Spatial. In Merrifield and Swyngedouw 1997.

Kelly, Lidia. 1999. South Phoenix Undergoing Rebirth. *The Arizona Re-public* 23 October: A1, A6.

Kennedy, Randall. 1997. *Race, Crime and the Law.* New York: Pantheon.

Kim, Suzin. 1996. Gangs and Law Enforcement: The Necessity of Limit-ing the Use of Gang Profiles. *The Boston Public Interest Law Journal* (Winter).

Kleiman, Mark, and Kerry Smith. 1990. State and Local Drug Enforce-ment: In Search of a Strategy. In *Drugs and Crime,* edited by Michael Tonry and James Q. Wilson. Chicago: University of Chicago Press.

Klein, Malcolm, Cheryl Maxson, and L. Cunningham. 1988. *Gang In-volvement in Cocaine Rock Trafficking: Final Report to the National Institute of Justice.* Los Angeles: University of Southern California.

Knowles, John, Nicola Persico, and Petra Todd. 1999. *Racial Bias in Motor Vehicle Searches: Theory and Evidence.* CARESS Working Paper #99-06.

Kocieniewski, David. 1999. Whitman Asks Delay in Case on Profiling. *New York Times* 6 March: B1, B5.

Konig, Ryan. 1997. Phoenix Plans to Cut Cruising. *The Arizona Republic* 28 November: B1, B3.

Kossan, Pat. 1996. Police To Close off Streets in S. Phoenix to Cruisers. *The Arizona Republic* 3 May 3: B1, B2.

Lait, Matt. 1999. Ganging Up on Gangs. *Los Angeles Times* 28 May 28: B2

Lamberth, John. 1996. Report in connection with the case *Wilkins v. Maryland State Police*, Civil Action No. CCB-93-483.

Lawrence, Charles, III. 1987. The Id, the Ego, and Equal Protection: Reckoning with Unconscious Racism. *Stanford Law Review* 39: 317.

Leadership Conference on Civil Rights. 2000. *Justice on Trial: Racial Disparities in the American Criminal Justice System*. Available on-line at http://www.civilrights.org/images/justice.pdf.

Leiber, Michael, Katherine Jamieson and Marvin Krohn. 1996. Newspaper Reporting and the Production of Deviance: Drug Use among Professional Athletes. In *Social Deviance: Readings in Theory and Research*, edited by H. Pontell. Englewood Cliffs, NJ: Prentice Hall.

Lelyveld, Nita. 1999. L.A. Officials Try To Cope as Police Scandal Spreads. *The Arizona Republic* 26 September: A6.

Lippard, Lucy R. 1990. *Mixed Blessings: New Art in Multicultural America*. New York: Pantheon.

Lipton, Jack P. 1983. Racism in the Jury Box: The Hispanic Defendant. *Hispanic Journal of Behavioral Sciences* 5: 275.

Lopez, Ian Haney. 2000. Institutional Racism Judicial Conduct and a New Theory of Racial Discrimination. *Yale Law Journal* 109(8): 1717.

Lopez, Robert J., and Rich Connell. 1999a. Police Probe Forces Suspension of Rampart Anti- Gang Injunction. *Los Angeles Times* 21 September: A24.

———. 1999b. Targets of Gang Injunctions Were Named by Officers in Police Probe. *Los Angeles Times* 23 September 23: A19.

Lowe, Fredrick H. 2000. Color-Tainted Policing. *One City*. Chicago: Council on Urban Affairs.

MacKenzie, Doris, and Craig Uchida, eds. 1994. *Drugs and Crime: Evaluating Public Policy Initiatives*. Thousand Oaks, CA: Sage.

MacLean, Brian, and Dragan Milovanovic, eds. 1990. *Racism, Empiricism, and Criminal Justice*. Vancouver: Collective Press.

Mann, CoraMae Richey. 1988. *Unequal Justice: A Question of Color*. Bloomington, IN: Indiana University Press.

———. 1990. Random Thoughts on the Ongoing Wilbanks-Mann Discourse. In MacLean and Milovanovic 1990.

———. 1993. *Unequal Justice: A Question of Color*. Bloomington, IN: Indiana University Press.

Massey, Douglas S., and Nancy A. Denton. 1993. *American Apartheid: Segregation and the Making of the Underclass.* Cambridge, MA: Harvard University Press.

Matsuda, Mari. 1996. *Where is Your Body?* Boston: Beacon Press.

Matsuda, Mari, Charles Lawrence III, Richard Delgado, and Kimberle Crenshaw, eds. 1993. *Words That Wound: Critical Race Theory, Assaultive Speech, and the First Amendment.* Boulder, CO: Westview Press.

Maxson, Cheryl. 1995. Research in Brief: Street Gangs and Drugs in Two Suburban Cities. In *The Modern Gang Reader,* edited by Malcolm Klein, Cheryl Maxson, and Jody Miller. Los Angeles: Roxbury.

Meehan, Patrick, and Patrick O'Carroll. 1992. Gangs, Drugs and Homicides in Los Angeles. *American Journal of Diseases of Children* 146: 638-687.

Merrifield, Andy, and Erik Swyngedouw, eds. 1997. *The Urbanization of Injustice.* New York: NYU Press.

Merrill, L. 1984. The Limits of Prosecutorial Summation. *South Texas Law Review* 1983-84: 629.

Miller, Jerome G. 1996. *Search and Destroy: African American Males in the Criminal Justice System.* New York: Cambridge University Press.

Milovanovic, Dragan, and Martin Schwartz. 1999. *Race, Gender and Class in Criminology: The Intersections.* New York: Garland.

Monk, R.C., ed. 1998. *Taking Sides: Clashing Views on Controversial Issues in Crime and Criminology.* 5th Edition. Dushkin Publishing: Guilford, Connecticut.

Mowatt, Raoul V. 1997. Gang Members' Rights Curbed by Court Ruling. *The Arizona Republic* 1 February: A1, A29.

Mumola, Christopher. 1998. *Substance Abuse and Treatment, State and Federal Prisoners, 1997.* Washington, D.C.: Bureau of Justice Statistics

Myrdal, Gunnar. 1944. *An American Dilemma: The Negro Problem and Modern Democracy.* New York: Harper and Row.

Newman, Andy. 1999. Court Upholds Extensive Stops of Black Men after a Crime. *New York Times* 27 October: B5.

O'Neill, Ann. 1995. Tagger's Killer Faces Firearms Charges. *Los Angeles Times* 24 February: B1,8.

Office of Applied Studies, Substance Abuse and Mental Health Services Administration. 1999. *Summary Findings from the 1998 Household Survey on Drug Abuse.* Rockville, MD: US Department of Health and Human Services.

Office of National Drug Control Policy. 1998. *Pulse Check: National Trends in Drug Abuse, Summer 1998.* Washington, D.C.: Office of National Drug Control Policy.

———. 1999. *National Drug Control Strategy 1999*. Washington, D.C.: Office of National Drug Control Policy.

Office of the New York State Attorney General. 2000. *The New York City Police Department "Stop and Frisk" Practices: A Report to the People of the State of New York from the Office of the Attorney General*.

Ogletree, Charles, Jr. 2000. The Role of Race in the U.S. Criminal Justice System and the Opportunities for International Responses. International Human Rights Law Group U.S. Racial Discrimination Program. Presented to the United Nations Commission on Human Rights, 56th Session, April 5, 2000 (Geneva, Switzerland).

Oliver, William. 1996. Reflection on Black Manhood. In *Images of Color: Images of Crime*, edited by Coramae Richie Mann and Majorie Zatz. Los Angeles: Roxbury.

———. Forthcoming. Cultural Racism and Structural Violence: Implications for African Americans. *Journal of Human Behavior in the Social Environment*.

Paik, Angela. 1999. Zero Tolerance Strikes a Chord Anti-Crime Message Works For Baltimore Nominee. *The Washington Post* 16 September.

Paul-Emile, Kimani. 1999. The Charleston Policy: Substance or Abuse? *Michigan Journal of Race and the Law* 4: 325.

Phillips, Susan A. 1999. *Wallbangin': Graffiti and Gangs in L.A.* Chicago: University of Chicago Press.

Poe-Yamagata, Eileen, and Michael A. Jones. 2000. *And Justice for Some: Differential Treatment of Minority Youth in the Justice System*. Washington, D.C.: Building Blocks for Youth.

Quindlen, Anna. 2000. The Problem of the Color Line: Here's the Riddle: Why Is Our Most Important Issue the One No One Really Wants to Talk About? *Newsweek* (135): 76.

Rabin, Jeffrey L. 1998. Officials Seek Injunction Against 92 Gang Members. *Los Angeles Times 5* May 5: B1, B3.

Reichel, Philip L. 1999. Southern Slave Patrols as a Transitional Police Type. *Policing Perspectives: An Anthology*. Los Angeles: Roxbury.

Reiman, Jeffrey. 1998. *The Rich Get Richer and the Poor Get Prison*. Boston: Allyn & Bacon.

Reinarman, Craig, and Harry Levine. 1997. The Crack Attack: Politics and Media in the Crack Scare. *Crack in America: Demon Drugs and Social Justice*. Berkeley: University of California Press.

Roberts, Dorothy E. 1999. Foreword: Race, Vagueness, and the Social Meaning of Order Maintenance Policing. *The Journal of Criminal Law and Criminology* 89: 3.

Rodriguez, Luis J. 1994. Los Angeles' Gang Culture Arrives in El Salvador, Courtesy of the INS. *Los Angeles Times* 8 May.

Rosen, Jeffery. 2000. A Look At . . . Zero Tolerance: When Good Policing Goes Bad. *The Washington Post* 23 April.

Rotenberg, Robert and Gary McDonogh, eds. 1993. *The Cultural Meaning of Urban Space.* Westport, CT: Bergin and Garvey.

Russell, Katheryn K. 1998. *The Color of Crime: Racial Hoaxes, White Fear, Black Protectionism and Police Harassment and Other Macroaggressions.* New York: New York University Press.

———. 1999. "Driving While Black": Corollary Phenomena and Collateral Consequences. *Boston College Law Review* 40(3): 717.

Sanchez-Tranquilino, Marcos. 1995. Space, Power, and Youth Culture: Mexican American Graffiti and Chicano Murals in East Los Angeles, 1972-1978. In Bright and Bakewell 1995.

Sandoval, Greg. 1997. Deputy Sentenced for Firing at Taggers, Lying on Report. *Los Angeles Times* 5 August: B2.

Savage, David G. 1999. Civil Liberties Back on the Street. *ABA Journal* 85: 50.

Schlosser, Eric. 1998. The Prison Industrial Complex. *The Atlantic Monthly* (December).

Schuman, Howard. 1991. Changing Racial Norms in America. *Michigan Quarterly Review* 30: 460.

Scott, Janny. 2000. Who Gets to Tell a Black Story? *New York Times* 11 June: A1.

Siegal, Nina. 1997. Ganging Up on Civil Liberties. *The Progressive* 61(10): 28-31.

Sigall, Harold, and Richard Page. 1971. Current Stereotypes: A Little Fading, a Little Faking. *Journal of Personality & Social Psychology* 18: 247.

Slade, David .S. 1999. Run! It's the Cops! Police: Protector or Enemy in High Crime Neighborhoods. *World and I* 14 (12): 86-89.

Smith, Eliot and Michael Zarate. 1990. Person Categorization and Stereotyping. *Social Cognition* 8: 161.

Smith, Tom and Glenn Dempsey. 1983. The Polls: Ethnic Social Distance and Prejudice. *Public Opinion Quarterly* 47: 584.

Soja, Edward W. 1989. *Postmodern Geographies.* London: Verso.

Stewart, Gary. 1998. Black Codes and Broken Windows: The Legacy of Racial Hegemony in Anti-Gang Civil Injunctions. *Yale Law Journal* (May).

Sugrue, Thomas J. 1996. *The Origins of the Urban Crisis: Race and Inequality in Postwar Detroit.* Princeton: Princeton University Press

Taylor, Ralph. 1999. Crime, Grime, Fear, and Decline: A Longitudinal Look. *National Institute of Justice Research in Brief* (July).

The New York Times. 1999. Los Angeles Courts Help Fight Gangs. (June 20): 27.

Tonry, Michael. 1995. *Malign Neglect: Race, Crime and Punishment in America.* New York: Oxford University Press.

U.S. Commission on Civil Rights. 2000. *Police Practices and Civil Rights in New York City.* Washington, D.C. Available at http://www.usccr.gov/nypolprc/main.htm.

U.S. Department of Justice, Federal Bureau of Investigation. 1998. *Uniform Crime Reports: Crime in the United States 1998.* Washington, D.C.: USGPO.

U.S. Department of State. 1999. *Initial Report of the United States of America to the United Nations Committee against Torture.* Washington, D.C.: USGPO.

U.S. General Accounting Office. 2000. *Better Targeting of Airline Passengers for Personal Searches Could Produce Better Results.* Washington, D.C.: USGPO.

U.S. Sentencing Commission. 1995. *Special Report to the Congress: Cocaine and Federal Sentencing Policy.* Washington, D.C.: USGPO.

———. 2000. *1999 Sourcebook of Federal Sentencing Statistics.* Washington, D.C.: USGPO.

van Dijk, Teun. 1987. *Communicating Racism: Ethnic Prejudice in Thought and Talk.* Newbury Park, CA: Sage.

Verniero, Peter and Paul Zoubek. 1999. *Interim Report of the State Police Review Team Regarding Allegations of Racial Profiling* (April 20). New Jersey Department of Law and Public Safety Publication.

Wallace, John and Jerald Bachman. 1991. Explaining Racial/Ethnic Differences in Adolescent Drug Use. *Social Problems* 38(3): 333-357.

Walsh, Michael. 1996. *Graffito.* Berkeley, CA: North Atlantic Books.

Weisburd, David and Lorraine Green. 1994. Defining the Street-Level Drug Market. In MacKenzie and Uchida 1994.

Weisheit, Ralph. 1992. *Domestic Marihuana: A Neglected Industry.* Westport, CT: Greenwood.

Werdegar, Matthew Mickle. 1999. Enjoining the Constitution: The Use of Public Abatement Injunctions against Urban Street Gangs. *Stanford Law Review* 51(2): 1-28.

White, Jack E. 1999. Endangered Species: The Police Component in Black-on-Black Crime. *Time* 153(1): 40.

Wilbanks, William. 1987. *The Myth of a Racist Criminal Justice System.* Monterey, CA: Brooks-Cole.

———. 1990. Response to the Critics of *The Myth of a Racist Criminal Justice System.* In MacClean and Milovanovic 1990.

Williams, Hubert, and Patrick Murphy. 1990. The Evolving Strategy of the Police: A Minority View. In *The Police and Society*, edited by Victor Kappeler. Illinois: Waveland Press.

Wilson, James Q. and George Kelling. 1982. Broken Windows: The Police and Neighborhood Safety. *The Atlantic* 249 (March).

Wisotsky, Steven. 1986. *Breaking the Impasse in the War on Drugs.* Westport, CT: Greenwood.

Wolpert, Carolyn. 1999. Considering Race and Crime: Distilling Non-Partisan Policy from Opposing Theories. *American Criminal Law Review* 36(2): 265-291.

Woodward, C. Vann. 1968. *The Strange Career of Jim Crow.* London: Oxford University Press.

Worden, Robert, Timothy Bynum, and James Frank. 1994. Police Crackdowns on Drug Abuse and Trafficking. In MacKenzie and Uchida (eds.) 1994.

Zatz, Majorie. 1990. A Question of Assumptions. In MacLean and Milovanovic 1990.

Zhao, Jihong. 1996. *Why Police Organizations Change: A Study of Community-Oriented Policing.* Washington, D.C.: Police Executive Research Forum.

Zinzun, Michael. 1997. The Gang Truce: A Movement for Social Justice. *Social Justice* 24(4): 258-266.

Zukin, Sharon. 1997. Cultural Strategies of Economic Development and Hegemony of Vision. In Merrifield and Swyngedouw 1997.

Contributors

Sandra Bass received her Ph.D. from University of California, Berkeley. Prior to coming to the University of Maryland, Dr. Bass spent a year as a postdoctoral fellow and researcher at the RAND Corporation in Santa Monica, California. While at RAND, Dr. Bass worked with a team of researchers on policing issues as well as violence prevention initiatives. She is currently working on a history of the Los Angeles Police Department to be published in June of 2001. Her current research interests include community policing, community building, the effects of personnel diversity on police organizations and police accountability.

Jackie Campbell teaches in the Department of Criminal Justice, Northeastern Illinois University. She is also a police officer (sergeant). She has a law degree from John Marshall. She has presented papers on the issue of race both at conferences as well as on campus.

Jeanette Covington is an Associate Professor in the Department of Sociology at Rutgers University in New Brunswick. In her research and publications, she has focused on the social ecology of crime, neighborhood change and crime, and fear of crime. She has also written and conducted research on the causes of drug use, the links between drug use and crime and our current drug policies. In her most recent work, she examines how criminologists construct the variable of "race" when analyzing data on crime and drugs.

Daniel Georges-Abeyie has a Ph.D. in the Geography of Crime, Law and Justice from Syracuse University. He is a professor of Administration of Justice at the Arizona State University West. Professor Georges-Abeyie teaches law enforcement and corrections. Dr. Georges-Abeyie's research interests include race and ethnic relations, forensic psychology, capital punishment, and minorities and the criminal justice system. Professor Georges-Abeyie's work has been published in numerous social science journals and edited volumes. He is the author/editor of three scholarly volumes, including a geopolitical novel, *The Red, The Green, the Black*. Dr. Georges-

Abeyie has been featured in numerous criminology and criminal justice videos.

Jeff Ferrell received his Ph.D. in Sociology from the University of Texas at Austin, and is currently a professor of Criminal Justice at Northern Arizona University. He is the author of *Crimes of Style: Urban Graffiti and the Politics of Criminality* (Garland, 1993; Northeastern University Press, 1996); author of *Tearing Down the Streets* (St. Martin's/Palgrave, 2001); editor, with Clinton R. Sanders, of *Cultural Criminology* (Northeastern University Press, 1995), the finalist for the American Society of Criminology's 1996 Michael J. Hindelang Award for Most Outstanding Contribution to Criminology; editor, with Mark S. Hamm, of *Ethnography at the Edge: Crime, Deviance, and Field Research* (Northeastern University Press, 1998); and editor, with Neil Websdale, of *Making Trouble: Cultural Constructions of Crime, Deviance and Control* (Aldine de Gruyter, 1999). He is the recipient of the 1998 Critical Criminologist of the Year Award, presented by the Critical Criminology Division of the American Society of Criminology.

Sheri Lynn Johnson is a Professor of Law and Co-Director of the Cornell Death Penalty Project at the Cornell Law School. Professor Johnson received her undergraduate degree from the University of Minnesota and her J.D. from the Yale Law School. Professor Johnson's scholarly interests focus on the role of race in the criminal process, and on the empirical study of the death penalty. Her work is most frequently cited in dissenting opinions. She works with the NAACP Legal Defense Fund to keep criminal defense attorneys up to date on developments in the litigation of racial justice issues. Professor Johnson represents inmates on death row in South Carolina and Georgia, and is committed to the abolition of the death penalty.

Dragan Milovanovic is Professor of Criminal Justice at Northeastern Illinois University. He is author of 14 books and contributes regularly to scholarly journals. In 1993 he received the "Distinguished Service Award" from the Division on Critical Criminology of the American Society of Criminology for his research and contributions to critical criminology. He is Editor of the *International Journals for the Semiotics of Law*. His recent works include: *Postmodern Criminology* (1997); *Chaos, Criminology and Social Justice* (1997); with Marty Schwartz, *Race, Gender and Class in Criminology: The Intersections* (1999); and with Stuart Henry, *Constitutive Criminology at Work* (1999).

Lee E. Ross is an Associate Professor of Criminal Justice at the University of Wisconsin-Parkside. A graduate of Rutgers University and a former federal law enforcement officer, he has published in the areas of crime and social control theory, self-esteem and delinquency, and more recently, the publication experiences of African-American criminologists. His reference book, *African American Criminologists, 1970-1996* broke new ground by focusing attention on neglected scholarship in criminal justice by African Americans. Recent publications concern racial profiling within the United States Customs Service. His work can be found in various journals, including *Justice Quarterly, The Criminologist, Sociological Focus, Sociological Spectrum*, the *Journal of Crime and Justice*, the *Journal of Criminal Justice*, and the *International Journal of Offender therapy* and *Comparative Criminology*, where he serves as Associate Editor.

Katheryn K. Russell is an Associate Professor of criminology and criminal justice at the University of Maryland, College Park. Dr. Russell received her undergraduate degree from the University of California, Berkeley, her law degree from Hastings Law School, and her Ph.D. from the University of Maryland. Her teaching, research and writing have been in the areas of criminal law, sociology of law, and race and crime. Her 1994 article, "The Constitutionality of Jury Override in Alabama Death Penalty Cases," published in the *Alabama Law Review*, was cited by the U.S. Supreme Court in *Harris v. Alabama* (1995). Dr. Russell's first book, *The Color of Crime*, was published by New York University Press (1998). She is at work on second book on race and crime.

Douglas E. Thompkins was awarded the American Society of Criminology Minority Fellowship in 1997, and a Ford pre-dissertation Fellowship in 1998. He attends the University of Illinois at Chicago, Department of Criminal Justice, where he currently writing his dissertation. His areas of research include the inmate social organization and the role of prisons in a global economy, the changing role of street gangs in a global economy and issues of youth violence.

Author Index

Subject Index